SLAVE WALES

Slave Wales

The Welsh and Atlantic Slavery, 1660–1850

CHRIS EVANS

UNIVERSITY OF WALES PRESS
CARDIFF
2010

British Library Cataloguing-in-Publication Data
A catalogue record for this book is available from the British Library.

ISBN 978-0-7083-2303-8
e-ISBN 978-0-7083-2304-5

Printed on demand by CPI Group (UK) Ltd, Croydon, CR0 4YY

Acknowledgements

Historians do not work alone. We rely upon the encouragement, bibliographical generosity and candour of others. Andy Croll, Neil Evans, E. Wyn James, Bill Jones and Göran Rydén have all helped here – some going so far as to read the whole manuscript.

The sections of this book that deal with Welsh-made 'Negro Cloth' have been improved by comments from Robert Protheroe Jones of the National Waterfront Museum and Ann Whitall of the National Wool Museum. Seth Brown shared his knowledge of US textile manufacturers who catered for slave markets without hesitation. Others have been equally quick to help with their knowledge of Cuba and Welsh-inspired copper mining there: Roger Burt, María Elena Díaz, Jonathan Curry-Machado, Lucy McCann at Rhodes House, Inés Roldán de Montaud, Robert Protheroe Jones (once again) and Sharron Schwartz.

Needless to say, those who have assisted me bear no responsibility for the arguments that I've made. Indeed, some are deeply sceptical.

Thanks also go to Bettina Harden and her co-workers at the Gateway Gardens Trust, the charity whose educational project on the links between Wales and slavery has been an inspiration. Grateful mention also goes to Nick Skinner of BBC Wales, whose invitation to participate in a programme on the 2007 bicentenary of the abolition of the British slave trade was the starting point for this book.

My research has only been possible because of the financial support offered by a number of bodies. I've been lucky enough to enjoy research fellowships at the Institute for Southern Studies at the University of South Carolina and the Virginia Historical Society, both of which contributed to this book. I've also been the beneficiary of research funding from the Historical Metallurgy Society and the Pasold Research Foundation. Above all, I've enjoyed the consistent support of the Faculty of Humanities and Social Sciences at the University of Glamorgan.

P. G. Wodehouse dedicated *Heart of a Goof*, his short story collection of 1926, to his adored step-daughter Leonora, 'without whose never-failing sympathy and encouragement this book would have been finished in half the time'. This book is dedicated to Ellis and Dan with the same wry affection.

Contents

The Atlantic slave system was so vast and endured over such a long period of time that it has no one history. It is a tangle of histories. There are few points on the ocean's circumference that did not feel the gravitational drag of slavery, but no two places felt it in the same way. Some locations participated very directly. They were the ports through which slaves passed or from which slave ships sailed. Some of these had a very prolonged involvement with the traffic in human beings. The export of slaves through Luanda on the Angolan coast, first documented in 1582, only ended in 1850. During those 268 years over 1.3 million men, women and children were embarked for the New World. Luanda's history as a slave port was an epic of suffering that few other places could match.

Other places had a far more distant or tangential connection to the world of slavery. Some connections are completely unexpected. Gammelbo, a tiny land-locked community in central Sweden, may seem as far removed from Atlantic slavery as it is possible to be in Europe, yet every summer in the 1730s and 1740s workmen at its four forges set aside their normal work and turned to making iron bars of very precise dimensions. Precision was important because these bars were exported via Stockholm to Bristol, sold there to slave merchants and then shipped on to West Africa where this so-called 'voyage iron' was used as a form of currency in slave markets. Just as some remote locations supplied commodities that could be exchanged for slaves, so others, even more distant, were recipients of slave labour. Black slaves first came to Peru in the 1530s with the Spanish conquistadors. By the end of the sixteenth century large numbers of Africans were being landed on the Caribbean coast of modern-day Colombia, trans-shipped across the Isthmus of Panama and then consigned to a second 'middle passage', over a thousand miles in length, down the west coast of South America. The ocean best known to the 20,000 Afro-Peruvian slaves living in Lima in 1640 was the Pacific, not the Atlantic.

Everywhere has a different tale to tell about the slave trade. Because the churning, slave-centred Atlantic economy was so immense it was also varied. It brought together regions that made highly specialised contributions. South-west Ireland, for example, became a major exporter of beef, butter and other salted provisions in the eighteenth century. The stimulus for Cork's rise as a meat-packing centre was quite specific: it was the escalating demand for barrelled beef to feed slaves in the Caribbean. A similar story can be told of many places in the Atlantic's hinterland (and some way beyond) that produced the things needed to buy slaves, or to feed them and clothe them. The fiercely salted beef of Munster joined linens from Silesia, muskets made in Liège, cottons from Gujerat, Clyde herrings, *cachaça* (the sugar-cane liquor of Bahia in Brazil) and much, much else besides in a huge swirl of commodities. The trade in Africans required them all.

So what of Wales? Direct involvement in the slave system – in the sense of fitting out slave voyages – was very limited. Wales was flanked by two of the largest slave ports in Europe – Bristol and Liverpool – but it is doubtful that a single slaving expedition left a Welsh harbour. (Not one of them had a merchant class of sufficient weight to raise the capital.) Nor did Wales contribute much in the way of maritime hardware to the slave Atlantic. A few Welsh-built ships did engage in the Guinea trade, but they were not many: just fourteen between the 1730s and the close of the legal trade in 1807. Of these, some made one-off contributions, like the *Nancy*, a 70-ton brig launched at Conway in 1755, which made a solitary venture into the trade. Departing Liverpool in July 1763, she was to land 131 Africans at St Kitts later that year.[1] Other vessels had more extended slaving careers. The 130-ton *John*, built at Milford Haven in 1765, made four slave voyages in the decade before the American Revolution. More than a thousand of her victims were delivered alive to the British sugar islands: 283 to Antigua, 266 to St Vincent, 245 to Dominica, others to Tobago, still others to Grenada.[2] But what did this amount to? A good many individual ports did more. The fourteen ships that are known to have been launched in Welsh yards (there may be others, of course, among the many whose place of construction is never specified in the official record) are outnumbered even by those of Newport, Rhode Island. Indeed, the colony of Rhode Island, a patch of New England coastline only one-fifth of the size of Wales, built over sixty slave ships in the course of the eighteenth century.

The part played by Wales in Atlantic slavery was oblique rather than direct, but it was nonetheless important. Eighteenth-century Wales was the source of certain commodities that were of considerable importance for the acquisition of slaves or that played a role in the lives of enslaved peoples in the Americas. By the same token, wealth accumulated in the slave trade or through the labour of coerced Africans had an impact on Wales. Its traces remain visible on the landscape. These issues are explored in the pages that follow. The Welsh dimension will be threaded through a broadly chronological narrative that follows the rise of England's slave empire in the mid-seventeenth century, through the heyday of the slave Atlantic in the eighteenth century, through the challenges to slavery that erupted at the end of the century and on to the stubborn vitality of the slave system in the nineteenth century, still flourishing across huge areas of the New World in the 1840s and 1850s. The events will be told from the perspective of Welsh actors.

The story begins in Santiago de Cuba in the 1660s; it concludes at the same Cuban city 180 years later.

E ven in 1662 Santiago de Cuba was an old town. Its founder, Diego Velázquez de Cuéllar, had sailed with Columbus in the fleet of 1493, the first European expedition to make landfall in Cuba. The city that Velázquez established in 1514 quickly became an important political and ecclesiastical centre, with handsome, stone-built public buildings and fine churches. It was (and remains) the seat of Cuba's archbishop. And it served as the island's capital for much of the sixteenth century. Hernán Cortés, the great conquistador, was an early mayor (*alcalde*); it was from Santiago that he set out for Mexico in 1519.

The English flotilla that appeared menacingly off Santiago de Cuba in October 1662 stood off, therefore, one of the Spanish empire's more important centres. On one of the eighteen ships under the command of Christopher Myngs was a young Welshman, Henry Morgan – or so most of Morgan's biographers have assumed. Hard evidence for the early life of the man who would become the most notorious freebooter of the age and the lieutenant-governor of Jamaica is hard to come by. Even so, it would have been extraordinary if Henry Morgan had not been present. He had come to the Caribbean as a soldier of fortune. He joined the growing band of privateers that operated out of Port Royal, Jamaica, hoping to get rich by raiding the Spanish Main. The Royal Navy provided the core of the fleet led by Vice-Admiral Christopher Myngs in the autumn of 1662, but the expedition also included every privateer fit for muster. That in itself suggests Morgan's participation. The speed, audacity and ruthlessness that Myngs showed in his assault is also suggestive, for here in embryo was the modus operandi that the Welshman would later make his own in sacking Portobello, Maracaibo and Panama. The attack on Santiago, whether witnessed first-hand or not, would certainly have taught Henry Morgan a contemptuous disregard for Spanish readiness.

The citizens of Santiago de Cuba would have felt no immediate alarm when the English fleet bore down on their coast. The wide bay on whose eastern shore the city sat could only be entered by a narrow twisting channel through which just one large vessel at a time could pass. It would be a rash commander who ran his ships under the guns of San Pedro de la Roca, the state-of-the-art fortress that occupied a promontory at the entrance to the channel. Christopher Myngs was a redoubtable, fighting captain, popular with his crews, but he was not rash. He chose a more oblique approach. Disembarking his men at a small and poorly defended wharf some miles to the east, he marched them without pause through the night. They fell upon a city whose garrison was in disarray and easily put to flight. Ten days were spent in plundering, reducing the cliff-top fortifications at San Pedro de la Roca, and – so the Spanish claimed – vandalising the cathedral, Cuba's oldest. This was a pattern that Henry Morgan would make his own, albeit with more emphasis on plunder. In the decade that followed the capture of Santiago de Cuba the privateers of Port Royal, under Morgan's command, would terrorise the coastal cities of Spanish America.

The Caribbean to which Henry Morgan came offered rich possibilities for a young man with a taste for violence and booty. The English had seized the island of Jamaica from the Spanish in 1655, the only significant outcome of Cromwell's 'Western Design', the ambitious naval thrust whose principal target had been the larger and richer island of Hispaniola. Jamaica was still largely uncultivated, its interior given over to trackless forest. But Jamaica's potential as a base for further offensive action against the Spanish empire was considerable, lying as it did astride the principal shipping routes that criss-crossed the Caribbean. The Anglo-Spanish war ended in 1660 – but only in Europe. For both sides there was 'no peace beyond the line'. The Spanish refused to recognise English possession of Jamaica and the English had no intention of halting their attacks on Spanish shipping and settlements. The harassment of Philip IV's empire was not carried out by regular naval forces, however; the task was left to licensed predators like Henry Morgan.

Morgan was a privateer, not a pirate. There was an important legal distinction between the two, although not one that Morgan's Spanish victims readily acknowledged. European states habitually issued privateering commissions to merchant captains in time of war, allowing them to intercept and seize enemy shipping. The taking-out of such a commission, a letter of marque, allowed attacks on ships flying the flag of a belligerent power – not shipping at large – and only in time of war. Any 'prizes' that were captured were submitted to an admiralty court to be condemned. Once condemned, the cargo and the vessel itself could be auctioned off and the proceeds shared out – a proportion going to the state, the remainder to be split amongst the privateers.

The privateer, in other words, operated within certain legal limits. Pirates did not. They raided indiscriminately, oblivious to peace treaties, formal declarations of war or other niceties. In the semi-lawless Caribbean of the 1650s and 1660s, however, reasons of state made the blurring of these distinctions convenient. Edward Doyley, Jamaica's governor from 1657 to 1662, was so conscious of the island's vulnerability to Spanish attack that he invited buccaneers from Tortuga to settle at Port Royal. Villainous though they were, they were a valuable deterrent. It was from their ranks, 1,500 strong by the early 1660s, that Henry Morgan recruited his crews.

This unstable and brutal world, into which Morgan stepped at some point *c.*1660, was one for which he was well prepared. Violence was his family's trade. Henry Morgan was born into the minor gentry of south-west Monmouthshire in the mid-1630s. The Llanrumney Morgans were a cadet branch of the rather more powerful Tredegar family of the same name. But whereas the Tredegar Morgans were an eminent county dynasty, their Llanrumney cousins were a far more modest, threadbare little clan. Short of acres, the Llanrumney Morgans dedicated themselves to the activity that was always open to men of lengthy pedigree but abbreviated rent rolls: the profession of arms. Several of Henry Morgan's uncles were career soldiers; both temperament and training pushed the future privateer in the same direction. He was, he later allowed, 'more used to the pike than the book' as a boy. Be that as it may, his sanguinary family background cannot in itself explain the extraordinary impact that Henry Morgan of Llanrumney had in the Caribbean. What Morgan also brought to Port Royal was charisma, cunning, a willingness to undertake missions that many hard-bitten members of the privateering fraternity baulked at, and abundant luck.

These qualities were evidently on display in the first expedition on which Henry Morgan was indisputably present: the raid
on the town of San Francisco de Campeche on the Yucatán coast
of Mexico and the prolonged and profitable incursion into
Central America that followed. Morgan was not listed as one of
the commanders who left Jamaica in 1663 but he returned as one
in 1665. Thereafter the Jamaican authorities smiled on Morgan
and issued a sequence of commissions to him, authorising him
to torment the Spanish in Cuba and elsewhere. And so began a
sequence of 'almost incredible Enterprizes and Successes'.[1]

The habit of command came naturally to Morgan and he
began to allow himself considerable latitude in interpreting the
terms of his commissions. Few could have anticipated the bold-
ness of his actions in attacking Portobello in July 1668. The city,
on the Caribbean side of the Isthmus of Panama, was a transit
point for Peruvian silver en route to the royal treasury in Spain.
Accordingly, it was strongly fortified and reputed to be impreg-
nable. It was not so. Henry Morgan stormed the fortifications
with a force that was just 500 strong; he incurred only eighteen
fatalities in doing so. A vicious saturnalia ensued. 'The Place now
being in their Power', Charles Leslie, the eighteenth-century
historian of Jamaica was to claim, 'they fell to their usual
Debaucheries, committed the most horrid Rapes and Murders,
tortured their Prisoners, and barbarously derided them in their
Miseries'.[2] The looting of the city realised between £70,000 and
£100,000 – more than the entire annual agricultural output of
Jamaica.

The sack of Portobello was a sensational exploit, giving the
man from Llanrumney, who was still in his early thirties, a notoriety that was European wide. He wasted no time in adding to
that reputation. Within a year he had laid waste to Maracaibo in
modern-day Venezuela, cannily evading what seemed certain
capture and death on his retreat. Then, in January 1671, he
launched a raid on Panama, Portobello's twin city on the Pacific
coast of the Isthmus. This was the most audacious of all his
undertakings. Over fifty miles of matted jungle separated
Morgan's objective from his Caribbean beachhead. Hacking
a path through the fetid tangle took seven days. The privateers

who staggered, ragged and rank, out of the forest were half-starved and much depleted by fever, but they were still too formidable a force for the civic militia that faced them. So secure from attack had Panama been assumed to be that it was not walled; so thorough and so traumatic was the destruction that Morgan visited upon the city that the site was abandoned and a new settlement, the present-day Panama City, built further down the coast.

The sack of Panama was Morgan's crowning achievement as a privateer. It brought him wealth (although the pickings were disappointingly small when compared to those of Portobello), honours (he was knighted in 1675) and political authority in Jamaica (he was appointed lieutenant-governor in 1674). In that sense Henry Morgan defined his era. Yet Morgan was also a transitional figure in the history of England's American empire. The imperial model he exemplified – predation upon the far larger Spanish empire – was not to endure. Indeed, even in Henry Morgan's heyday there were many who argued for a different model, one based upon a grudging co-existence with the Spanish. Advocates of this view acknowledged that the privateering at which Morgan excelled could bring immense profits, but profits that were irregular and unpredictable. Moreover, as with any military enterprise, defeat was always a possibility, and failure meant the writing-off of almost everything invested in an expedition. Was it not better to opt for the less spectacular but more certain gains that could be had from trade? Especially the trade in slaves?

There had long been a ready market for slaves in Spanish America. They had been used extensively in both Peru and Mexico since the sixteenth century. Some 135,000 captive Africans were landed at the Caribbean port of Cartagena between 1595 and 1640, most of them for transhipment to Peru. Another 70,000 were inducted into bondage in Mexico on the quayside at Veracruz; 44,000 more were disembarked at Buenos Aires. The *asiento* – the licence to supply the Spanish empire – was a highly lucrative prize, one that rival Portuguese and Dutch cartels periodically wrestled over. The *asiento* also caught the eye of British merchants, a group of whom were incorporated by royal charter in 1663 as the 'Company of Royal Adventurers of England trading with Africa'. The company's regal title was more than ornament. Shareholders included Charles II himself, Catherine of Braganza, his queen, the duke of York (the future James II) and Prince Rupert of the Rhine, the royalist hero of the civil wars. Members of the landed elite, scenting a politically secure investment opportunity, followed the royal example. Henry Morgan's wealthy cousins, the Morgans of Tredegar Park, were among them.[3] Favour at court secured the adventurers (reconstituted in 1672 as the Royal African Company) a monopoly of trade with Guinea: ivory, gold, hardwoods, pepper and, of course, slaves. But for this monopoly to be fully exploited, peace with Spain was desirable.

The political tide of the 1670s was turning against the privateers. They continued to enjoy the indulgence of Henry Morgan, who remained a force to be reckoned with as a magistrate at Port Royal, but even in Jamaica voices were raised against the doctrine of 'no peace beyond the line'. In the first years of English occupation Jamaica had kept the character of a military frontier. Little of the island was cleared for cultivation and much of the north coast was left unsettled for fear of Spanish attack. Slowly, however, the possibilities of plantation agriculture became apparent. A new governor, John Vaughan, arrived in 1674 with instructions to expedite sugar planting. He was soon at odds with Morgan and his pro-buccaneering faction. A power struggle between the two Welshmen ensued. (Vaughan was MP for Carmarthen and later for the Carmarthenshire county seat.) Morgan was the more popular man on the island but the logic of economic development favoured John Vaughan and the planters' clique on the island's council. In 1671 there were just 57 sugar plantations on Jamaica; by 1685 there were 246. Meanwhile the number of privateers operating out of Port Royal drifted slowly downwards: the 2,000 or so cut-throats of 1671 had dwindled to 1,200 by 1689. In the same period the number of slaves on the island vaulted up from 2,500 to 25,000. The sugar revolution had swept Jamaica.

The system of sugar cultivation that was to dominate the Atlantic in the seventeenth and eighteenth centuries – and which was to be the chief motor of Atlantic slavery – first achieved recognisable form on the equatorial African island of São Tomé, which the Portuguese seized in the 1470s. Sugar was already being raised in the Azores and Madeira in the mid-fifteenth century, but by organisationally varied methods and with a mixed workforce of wage labourers, indentured servants and African captives. To the Portuguese of São Tomé belongs the dubious credit of developing a wholly slave-based system of sugar production. Its key features were monoculture (other crops were suppressed as a distraction), large-scale production, total reliance on slave labour, a highly regimented work regime and heavy investment in sophisticated processing equipment. This mass mobilisation of enslaved labour, coupled with lavish fixed capital, gave the nascent sugar plantation an industrial character. Appropriately enough, the Portuguese word for the milling machinery at the centre of every plantation, *engenho* (engine), was soon used to denote the plantation as a whole.

The sugar plantation entered Atlantic circulation in the sixteenth century. By the 1550s the Portuguese had implanted the São Tomé model in north-east Brazil. It was immediately successful: sixty *engenhos* were at work in Pernambuco in the 1580s and a further forty in Bahia. So successful was the Brazilian sugar industry that it attracted the covetous attention of the Dutch. The foundation of the *Westindische Compagnie* in Amsterdam in 1621 signalled the beginning of a determined attempt to oust the Portuguese from their South American sugar colonies. The Dutch enjoyed initial good fortune. Pernambuco was overrun in 1630 and rechristened New Holland. The African forts through which the Portuguese funnelled slaves westward were also targeted. Elmina on the Gold Coast capitulated to a *Westindische Compagnie* fleet in 1637; the trading stations in Angola followed suit in 1641. For the next quarter of a century the Dutch were the masters of the south Atlantic sugar-slave network.

The Portuguese regrouped, however, and managed to expel the Dutch from Brazil in 1654. The fall of New Holland had major consequences. Refugees streamed north to Dutch settlements in Surinam and to Caribbean islands like Curacao and Sint Eustatius. They took with them the plantation model perfected on Pernambuco's *engenhos*. They also carried off hundreds of slaves who had been drilled in the Brazilian methods of sugar cultivation. The advanced production techniques were not long restricted to the Dutch islands. They were taken up by the French and English on the volcanic specks that they had recently occupied in the Lesser Antilles: Guadeloupe and Barbados. And from there they spread to Jamaica. Packs of white Barbadians descended on Jamaica, intent on seizing the island's virgin soil. Recurrent wars with the Dutch allowed the seizure of much else besides. When Henry Morgan's uncle, Sir Thomas Morgan, led a raiding party to Sint Eustatius, the veteran Welshman's troops made off with '900 slaves ... with many coppers and stills to the great furtherance of the colony [in Jamaica]'.[4] These were 'very brave knowing blacks', schooled in the Pernambucan ways of growing cane.

It was the way of the future, as even Henry Morgan had to concede. In the last decade of his life the arch-privateer became a planter, buying 1,190 acres in St Mary's parish on Jamaica's north coast. He called his plantation Llanrumney.

Llanrumney, like any other plantation, required slaves. Lavish quantities of human labour had to be applied if the high-volume, high-pressure sugar production system was to work effectively. The number of labourers needed greatly exceeded the number of potential migrants from the British Isles in the last decades of the seventeenth century. Besides, the work routine was so harsh and the Caribbean disease environment so notoriously deadly for Europeans that few who had any choice would volunteer for the task. Forced labour was the only option.

Various stop-gaps were tried in the mid-seventeenth century, European convicts and prisoners of war among them, but their numbers were nowhere near adequate. Enslaved Africans held more promise. If there were legal and cultural obstacles to the mass enslavement or deportation of Europeans they did not apply to the visibly different and culturally alien inhabitants of sub-Saharan Africa. The Portuguese were the pioneers. They began to traffic in Africans in the 1440s. The earliest slaves were sent back to Portugal itself, to Lisbon or to the large agricultural estates of the Algarve. By the sixteenth century, however, a transatlantic trade had opened up. The first documented slave voyage to the Americas was in 1525. There would be nearly 35,000 others before the trade finally closed in the 1860s. In the sixteenth century and the first half of the seventeenth slave transports went overwhelmingly to Spain's empire on the American mainland or to Brazil. The Caribbean islands were of marginal importance. Just 15,000 slaves were landed alive between 1601 and 1650. The picture was very different in the fifty years that followed, when the sugar revolution swept through the world of Henry Morgan. Between 1651 and 1700 over 352,000 slaves were disembarked on what were now the sugar islands.

The transatlantic slave trade had come to a horrible maturity. It was now a vast enterprise. The movement of millions of captives was achieved with the aid of a powerful infrastructure (docks, forts, victualling depots), elaborate supply chains and sophisticated financial mechanisms. What the English called the 'Guinea Trade' was at the commercial and technological cutting edge. Its complexities and its risks, not to mention its cruelties, are hinted at in the history of one particular voyage, the one that took the *Hannibal* to Barbados in 1693–5. Although the *Hannibal* sailed from London its owner and its captain were both Welshmen.

Jeffrey Jeffreys was a merchant of eminence in late Stuart London, prosperous and politically well connected. He traded to the Chesapeake and the Caribbean, carrying Virginian tobacco and sugar from the Leeward Islands to European markets. As befitted someone who dealt in slave-produced commodities, he also engaged in the Guinea trade. And he did so in no small way, for he was an 'Assistant' – a director – of the Royal African Company.

Although he moved in exalted metropolitan circles, Sir Jeffrey – he was knighted in 1699 after his election as sheriff to the City of London – was not a native of the capital. His ancestral home was at Llywel in Brecknockshire, beneath the scarp of the Black Mountains. And he retained Welsh links; indeed, he nurtured them. The purchase of The Priory estate in Brecon gave Jeffreys considerable heft locally, leading to his return as MP for the borough between 1690 and 1698 and between 1701 and his death in 1709. Like any attentive political patron, he sought to advance the careers of local men. One of these was Captain Thomas Phillips, a mariner whose fortunes had dipped after his last command was intercepted by French men-of-war in the early days of the Nine Years War (1689–98). A period of detention in Brest was the outcome. Eventually, though, Phillips made his way back to London:

> After my return to *England* I was for some time destitute of employ-
> ment, until my ever honoured patron and benefactor, Sir *Jeffrey Jeffreys*,
> Knt. out of his extraordinary generosity and good will to me, under-
> standing that the ship *Hannibal,* of four hundred and fifty tons, and
> thirty-six guns, was to be sold, gave me orders to buy her.[1]

Phillips was to take a part-share in the vessel, but most of the capital was to be advanced by Jeffreys and his cronies. These included Jeffreys's younger brother John, MP for Radnorshire and another assistant of the Royal African Company, and Sir Samuel Stanier, a sub-governor of the company. These connec-tions were put to immediate use; the *Hannibal* was chartered by the Royal African Company for 'a trading voyage to *Guiney,* for elephants teeth, gold, and Negro slaves'. In doing this, Jeffrey Jeffreys was following a pattern set by his uncle, John Jeffreys (*c*.1614–88) of Llywel, whose business fortune he had inherited. Uncle John had been an assistant of the Royal African Company too, and had imported large numbers of slaves into Virginia in the 1670s and 1680s under license from the company. Details of the slaving expeditions fitted out by Uncle John are sketchy. The voyage of the *Hannibal*, on the other hand, is very well documented, for Captain Thomas Phillips wrote a lengthy memoir of his command.

The *Hannibal* cleared Gravesend in September 1693 and joined a convoy of ships bound for Africa: the *East-India Merchant* of thirty guns; the twenty-four-gun *Mediterranean*, which was sailing to Angola; the twelve-gun *Fortune*, also heading to Angola; the *Jeffrey* of twelve guns, with orders for the Bight of Benin; and the *Eagle* packet, which was bound for the Gambia. The *Hannibal* was destined for the Gold Coast, the main area of activity for the Royal African Company. Captain Phillips had on board thirty-three employees of the company – mainly soldiers – who were to be delivered to Cape Coast Castle, the company headquarters, as well as seventy crewmen.

The voyage did not go smoothly. Squalls dispersed the little convoy bit by bit as it left the English Channel. Then the *Hannibal*'s mizzen mast snapped in a gale and a seaman was lost overboard as the crew struggled to bring the pitching vessel under control. Worse was to threaten as Thomas Phillips steered past the Canary Islands. On 23 November 1693 the *Hannibal* was attacked by the *Louis*, a French privateer of fifty-two guns. A stiff engagement followed, as the two ships exchanged broadsides from four in the afternoon until ten at night. The French aggressor was eventually driven off, but the *Hannibal* was 'most miserably shatter'd and torn in her mast and rigging'. As for her crew, there were 'five men killed out-right and about thirty-two wounded'. Nevertheless, the *Louis* had been worsted: 'I never heard such dreadful screeching and howling as was on board of him, so that he must needs have a great many men wounded.'[2]

The days that followed were spent in plugging holes in the hull, patching up the tattered sails and amputating limbs. It was with relief that Phillips sighted the first of the Cape Verde islands, 300 miles off the western-most tip of Africa. The *Hannibal* put in at Praia, the chief port of the archipelago, to pick up fresh water and provisions. This scatter of Portuguese-controlled rocks, though sun-baked and largely barren, acted as a staging-post for vessels of all sorts, as Phillips noted: 'They lie very convenient for the refreshment of shipping in their way to *Guiney* or the *East Indies*, and [there are] few *English*, *Dutch*, or *French East Indiamen* but call here outward-bound.'[3] As 1693 drew to a close the *Hannibal* struck out south and east, encountering wild electrical storms as she sailed on. Captain Phillips was not disheartened: the tempests and waterspouts were a sign that the African coast was near. Sure enough, three days before Christmas, at eight in the morning, Cape Mount in modern-day Liberia was sighted.

A day later, having travelled about fifty miles down the coast, Captain Phillips found a number of sails at anchor in the roads off Cape Mesurado. One was the *East-India Merchant*, part of the convoy that had been lost sight of weeks earlier; another was 'an interloper come from *Barbadoes*'. Although the Royal African Company enjoyed a legal monopoly on English trade on the coast of Guinea, a swarm of illegal traders ('interlopers') infringed upon it, attracted by the premium prices that African commodities commanded and confident that the company lacked the coercive edge to enforce its legal rights. The vessel commanded by Captain Gubbins was one such. She was 'chiefly laden with rum, to trade for gold and slaves'. Thomas Phillips was a legitimate trader, licensed by the Royal African Company. Even so, rum could lubricate his own dealings along the coast, so he bought 500 gallons from Gubbins and later 'sold it to good advantage'.

It was at Cape Mesurado, the site of the present-day city of Monrovia, that Captain Phillips encountered his first Africans. 'The people here are civil and courteous, but great beggars, the king and his cappashiers [courtiers] continually haunting us for dashes (which is their word for presents).'[4] It was here too that Phillips began to learn the etiquette of trade on the Guinea coast.

If African goods were to be obtained, certain protocols had to be observed and local tastes attended to. First and foremost, local rulers had to be appeased with elaborate displays of respect. The firing of cannon, toasting with punch and brandy, feasting and the distribution of 'dashes' were essential preliminaries to commerce. Phillips's priorities were timber with which to repair his masts and a bulk foodstuff with which to feed the human captives he planned to take on board further to the east. Both were readily available. The coastal forest had 'trees of that size as will mast a 700 ton ship', while 'vast quantities of rice' were grown on the floodplains of the Windward Coast's mangrove-fringed rivers. Phillips bought five tons of rice, 'paying mostly for it in booges or cawries, which are the goods they most esteem'.[5] Cowries or 'booges' (a corruption of the Portuguese *búzios*) were mollusc shells that were widely used as a currency in Atlantic Africa. As soon 'as the negroes have them they bore holes in the backs of them, and string them on rushes, 40 shells on each, which they call a foggy: and five of such foggys being tied together, is call'd a galina'.[6] Phillips reported this as a curiosity, but there was nothing irrational in it. Cowries had many of the attributes of a precious metal. The supply was limited – cowries were the durable part of a marine organism restricted to certain parts of the Indian Ocean – and they were impossible to counterfeit. They did not break; they did not perish. And like gold and silver they could be used decoratively: glossy and smooth, cowries were frequently incorporated into ceremonial costume.

The inhabitants of this part of the Windward Coast were also keen to acquire 'iron bars and red *Welsh* plains'. The *Hannibal* was carrying both as a matter of course. Iron and Welsh plains were part of the standard consignment of goods that the Royal African Company despatched to its factors. Voyage iron – 'the only sort and size used throughout all *Nigritia, Guinea,* and *West-Æthiopia,* in the way of trade' – was widely employed as a currency in African slave marts.[7] The African Company was exporting about 10,000 bars annually by the early 1680s. Voyage iron was manufactured to exact specifications: every bar was to be of a set length, 'with [the maker's] Mark or Marks on each Barr and the

Number to be from 75 to 80 Barrs at the least in each tun', as the company insisted to a supplier.[8] They were specially made in Sweden. 'Welsh plains' were coarse woollens. They were made, naturally enough, in Wales.

In January 1694 the *Hannibal* continued down the coast to the river Sanguin, which marked the beginning of the Grain Coast. The grains that gave this stretch of the coast its name were not cereal, they were the seed-pods of the malagueta pepper, much sought after by slavers. 'The reason of our buying this pepper', Phillips explained, 'is to give our negroes in their messes to keep them from the flux and dry belly-ach, which they are very incident to.'[9] It was not to be so. When, in due course, the *Hannibal*'s human cargo was devastated by the 'flux', the pepper's therapeutic powers were unavailing. The most immediate concern of Captain Phillips, however, was not the health of his as yet unbought slaves; it was the health of his crew. The *Hannibal* had entered an equatorial disease environment, one to which his European crew were unaccustomed. Slowly, they began to succumb to tropical fevers. One of the first to sicken was Phillips's own brother, a junior officer on the *Hannibal*. He died after eight days of fevered delirium in January 1694 and was buried at sea off Cape Palmas, with 'our trumpets and drums sounding and beating, as is customary of such melancholy occasions ... the *Hannibal* fired sixteen guns at 1/2 minute distance of time, which was the number of years he had liv'd in this uncertain world'.[10] The doleful boom of cannon was to become very familiar as, one after another, Phillips's crewmen fell victim to the 'same distemper' that had claimed their commander's brother.

Rounding Cape Palmas, the *Hannibal* began to travel east along the Ivory Coast. The buying of ivory was a major consideration for Phillips. Indeed, in the late seventeenth century 'teeth', and to a still greater extent gold, loomed large in England's Guinea trade; it was only in the eighteenth century that human flesh became the dominant constituent in Anglo-African commerce. Tusks were brought out to the *Hannibal* in canoes, but somewhat warily. The Africans required Phillips to 'come down the out side of the ship, and drop three drops of sea water into his eye, as a pledge of friendship'. Phillips was no less shy of his guests, eyeing nervously their filed teeth, plaited hair and body paint. Unlike their counterparts on the Grain Coast, the traders here had little taste for cowries, nor for Welsh plains. 'The goods they most covet are pewter basons, the large the better, iron bars, knives, and large screw'd pewter jugs.'[11]

The *Hannibal* skirted the reefs off Cape Three Points on 16 February 1694 and began her cruise along the Gold Coast, modern-day Ghana. The African coastline that Phillips had navigated up to this point was thickly forested, but to the east of Cape Three Points the forests thinned, allowing for easy communications with the inland savannah regions. It was fortunate that access to the interior was relatively trouble free, because extensive gold deposits were to be found to the north. It was the availability of gold at a rate below which it exchanged in Europe that had aroused Portuguese interest in this area in the fifteenth century. The possibility of obtaining African gold by a direct sea route, thereby dispensing with the services of the Arab intermediaries whose caravans had brought the metal across the Sahara in the middle ages, had been a spur to Portuguese navigation.

It was the Portuguese who established the first permanent European presence on the Gold Coast in 1481, when a local African ruler was persuaded to allot them a beachside patch on which to construct a fortified trading post. It was christened São Jorge da Mina – or Elmina to give its shorthand title. The Portuguese were the pioneers, but by the seventeenth century the Gold Coast – unlike the shoreline to west and east, where there were no enduring European encampments – was studded with forts belonging to the Dutch, the Danes, the English, the French and the Brandenburg Germans. Many of the forts were within sight of one another, so dense was the pattern of settlement.

Elmina was in the hands of the Dutch when Thomas Phillips anchored off this surf-lashed coast. They had evicted the Portuguese in 1637 during the epic struggle for control of the south Atlantic sugar-slave network. Whereas the Portuguese had succeeded in retaking Brazil and the slave ports of Angola, the

Dutch hung on to Elmina, making it the African headquarters of the *Westindische Compagnie*. The principal English fort lay a dozen miles or so to the east: Cape Coast Castle. The castle on *Cabo Corso* ('the short cape' in Portuguese, which was anglicised into Cape Coast) was of a more recent vintage. The Swedes had first built upon the spot in 1655, but before long they were ousted by the Danes, whose own tenure was ended by the Dutch. Cape Coast then fell to the English in 1664. Such rapid reversals were not uncommon in the seventeenth century as Europeans jock-eyed for position and the favour of African rulers. The English conquest of 1664 was to prove lasting, however. The Royal African Company retained control for the remainder of the slave era.

Cape Coast Castle was the African Company's command centre, to which all other forts on the coast were subordinate. 'This castle', Phillips recorded, 'has a handsome prospect from the sea, and is very regular and well-contriv'd fortification, and as strong as it can be made . . . being encompass'd with a strong and high brick wall.' Bastions projected at each corner. The walls enclosed a 'fine spacious square wherein 4 or 500 men may be very conveniently drawn up and exercised'. These imposing defences were not primarily intended for protection against the local population. Although the shifting politics of the region offered no guarantee of security, the major danger came from rival European powers, not from hostile Africans. Cape Coast Castle, after all, existed at the sufferance of the local potentate, the dey of Efutu, to whom a rent was paid. Most of the castle's cannon pointed out to sea, 'where they would do good execution upon any ships that should pretend to attack', as Phillips noted with grim satisfaction.[12]

The castle community was sizeable. The civil population was headed by the chief agent, who handled all the dealings in gold. He was assisted by a warehouse-keeper and a book-keeper. A chaplain and a surgeon attended to the spiritual and medical welfare of the company's men. European tradesmen with indis-pensable skills – armourers, smiths and carpenters – added to the total. The military garrison was a hundred strong. Most of the inhabitants were Africans, however. The 'Castle slaves' were porters, cooks, washerwomen and labourers. The Africans made up the more stable part of the castle's population. The Europeans were by nature impermanent. They were destined to shift from one fort to another as opportunities for promotion emerged, or they would eventually find their way home. Equally likely, however, was the possibility of finding a home in the castle cemetery. Englishmen who did not quickly acclimatise perished at a fearsome rate. Thomas Phillips could testify to that:

> We landed out of the *Hannibal* at this place thirty soldiers of the company, in as good health as we receiv'd them aboard in *England*; but in two months time that we lay here to compleat our business, they were near half dead, and scarce enough of the survivors able to carry their fellows to the grave.

It was no doubt a consciousness of the fragility of life that led Europeans at the castle to consume alcohol and rich foods with an avidity that was out of the ordinary even in an age that admired indulgence at the table. A sense of transience must also have contributed to the rapid turnover of native concubines among the castle's officers that so struck visitors.

The *Hannibal* had come to Cape Coast Castle primarily to accumulate gold, not slaves. Captain Phillips did a busy trade through March and April 1694, welcoming African merchants on board, treating them with punch and brandy, but taking care that brass filings and other adulterants had not been mixed in with the gold dust that was offered for sale. The principal goods that the local traders wanted in return were textiles: perpetuanos from Devon and sayes from East Anglia. (Welsh plains, on the other hand, had no takers.) Having bought a sufficient quantity of gold, Phillips quit Cape Coast Castle on 25 April 1694 with the usual gun salutes. The *Hannibal* tracked down the coast to the Royal African Company's factory at Anomabu, where 140 chests of maize were taken on board, then on to the lodge at Winneba. The African Company's fort at Accra, where further chests of maize were loaded, was the *Hannibal*'s last port of call on the Gold Coast. Passing the mouth of the river Volta at midnight on 18 May 1694 Captain Phillips entered upon the Slave Coast.

The *Hannibal* anchored off Whydah on the Bight of Benin thirty-six hours later. Stretching back from the coast was 'the pleasantest country I have seen in Guiney', Phillips wrote, 'consisting of champaigns and small ascending hills, beautify'd with always green shady groves of lime, wild orange, and other trees, and irrigated with divers broad fresh rivers'.[13] The shore-line itself, though, was laced with swamps and malarial lagoons, and it was in this insalubrious setting that the Royal African Company's fort was set down.

> The factory is ... a most wretched place to live, by reason of the swamps adjacent, whence proceed noisome stinks, and vast swarms of little flies, call'd musketoes, which are so intolerably troublesome, that if one does not take opium, laudanum, or some other sopor-ifick, 'tis impossible to get any sleep at night.[14]

It was also intensely hot; so oppressive was the atmosphere, Phillips continued, that it was 'as if he had suck'd in the heat at the mouth of an oven in *England*'. In these appropriately hellish surroundings the *Hannibal* was readied for the 700 terrified human beings who were to be carried to Barbados.

Before slaves could be purchased, however, proper obeisance had to be shown to the local ruler. Together with the Royal African Company's chief factor at Whydah and the captain of the *East-India Merchant*, with whom he was still keeping company, Thomas Phillips was carried by hammock to the royal palace:

> When we were enter'd, the king peep'd upon us from behind a curtain, and beckon'd us to him; whereupon we approach'd close to his throne, which was ... surrounded with dirty old curtains, always drawn 'twixt him and his cappasheirs, whom he will not allow the sight of his handsome phiz.[15]

The audience was accompanied, as ever, with a sequence of toasts 'in brandy, and pitto, which is a pleasant liquor made of *Indian* corn'. As a meal of stewed fowl was served, the king professed his great love for the Royal African Company. The company's men responded in the expected fashion, promising 'to present him with blunderbusses, silks *&c.* which we had from the royal *African* company for that purpose'.[16] With these civilities concluded, the terms of trade could be discussed and price schedules agreed. At Whydah, as at other markets, a very specific basket of goods was required. Cowries ('the smaller the more esteem'd') were essential. 'The next in demand are brass neptunes or basons, very large, thin and flat.' Certain textiles were also acceptable ('sletias, cambricks or lawns, caddy chints'), but only to a limited extent: 'near half the cargo value must be cowries or booges, and brass basons, to set off the other goods'.[17]

On 21 May 1694, ten months after the *Hannibal* had set sail from the Thames, the buying of slaves began. The human merchandise was stored at a lock-up known as the trunk: 'an old house where all the slaves are kept together, and evacuate nature where they lie, so that no jakes can stink worse'. When Captain Phillips and his party arrived 'the king's slaves, if he had any, were the first offer'd for sale'. It was not politic to refuse them, though 'they were generally the worst slaves in the trunk'. Every potential purchase was examined by the *Hannibal*'s surgeon 'to see that they were sound wind and limb, making them jump, stretch out their arms swiftly, looking in their mouths to judge of their age', and inspecting them closely for signs of the yaws, the tropical disease that was endemic on the coast. Those selected were branded 'in the breast, or shoulder, with a hot iron, having the letter of the ship's name on it'.[18]

Once a sufficient number of slaves had been chosen, and payment made to the 'captain of the trunk', they were marched the seven miles to the sea under the supervision of the 'captain of slaves'. (Another African official, the 'captain of the sand', was responsible for conveying European goods inland.) For most of the captives this was their first sight of the ocean and the giant European ships that lay offshore. Panic overcame them as they were thrust into canoes, 'they having a more dreadful apprehension of *Barbadoes* than we do of hell'. Numbers 'leap'd out of the canoes ... into the sea, and kept under water till they were drowned, to avoid being taken up and saved by our boats'.[19] A dozen evaded the fate in store for them in this way, but for most the ride out through the Atlantic swell – itself a nightmare of spume-drenched rearing and plunging – was ruthlessly policed. Security was also paramount when the slaves were received on the *Hannibal*. The men were put in irons without delay, 'two and two shackled together, to prevent their mutiny, or swimming ashore'. Awaiting them were '30 or 40 gold coast negroes, which we buy, and are procur'd there by our factors, to make guardians and overseers of the *Whidaw* negroes'. The 'guardians', each of whom carried a 'cat of nine tails as a badge of his office', were charged with keeping order among the newcomers, and to 'give us notice, if they can discover any caballing or plotting among them, which trust they will discharge with great diligence'.[20] In the event of an insurrection the crew stood ready: 'we always keep centinels upon the hatchways, and have a chest of small arms, ready loaden and prim'd, constantly lying at hand … together with some grenada shells; and two of our quarter-deck guns, pointing on the deck'.[21]

Slave captains well understood that as long as they remained anchored in sight of the African coast their captives clung to the slim hope of freeing themselves. Uprisings were far less common once a ship had put to sea and slaves were confronted by a horizon of limitless salt water. For that reason, slavers did not linger. Yet filling the below decks of a ship of the *Hannibal*'s size was no easy matter. Phillips had capacity for 700 slaves; the *East-India Merchant*, which was also loading at Whydah, had orders for 650 more. Even with regular replenishment at the trunk, this took time, although Phillips was to claim that if the supply of slaves was particularly tight the king would obligingly sell up to 400 of his wives to expedite business. It was not until 27 July, after sixty-eight days of trading, that the *Hannibal* had her full complement.

Barbados now beckoned. But Thomas Phillips did not immediately turn to the west. On the contrary, he bore east and south, heading for São Tomé. There was method, not madness, in this. The *Hannibal* was packed with over 750 people, and a prodigious quantity of fresh water would be needed to keep them alive. This was what São Tomé could provide. The island sat directly on the equator, with mountain peaks that were shrouded in cloud. A continuous drizzle in the highlands fed a multitude of streams, affording an abundant supply of water. São Tomé's rich volcanic soil made the island a good source of fresh provisions as well: maize, kidney beans, plantains, yams, potatoes and citrus fruit.

Captain Phillips took full advantage of this plenty, spending four-teen days re-victualling. Hoisting the great casks of sweet water aboard took until 25 August 1694. Only then did Phillips give orders for the *Hannibal* to sail for the Caribbean. The Middle Passage had commenced.

The Middle Passage stands as the central horror of Atlantic slavery. It was an ordeal for which the *Hannibal*'s inmates were ill prepared. Many had already spent weeks on debilitating marches from slave markets hundreds of miles inland. Those who were amongst the first batches to be bought by Thomas Phillips had then to spend upwards of two months in the stifling confines of the slave decks waiting for the *Hannibal* to embark on the Middle Passage proper. Conditions on board deteriorated steadily as every available inch was used to accommodate the hundreds of prisoners who were ferried out from the beach. It was easy enough for disease to take hold of a shipboard population that was physically weakened, psychologically traumatised and kept in conditions of enforced intimacy in which aggressive bacteria could flourish. Even as the *Hannibal* lay off São Tomé slaves were dying at the rate of two or three a day. Far worse was to come.

Slave mortality was a matter of keen interest to slave ship commanders. The profitability of a voyage rested upon mini-mising the death rate. Some basic steps were therefore taken to preserve the livestock – for that is how the enslaved were viewed. Exercise and good diet were prescribed. Every evening groups of slaves were brought up 'into the sun to air themselves'; they were forced to 'jump and dance for an hour or two to our bag-pipes, harp, and fiddle'. This phoney revel concluded, the slaves were driven back 'to their kennels below deck'.[22] As for diet, the daily ration on the *Hannibal* was a maize-based gruel called 'dabbadabb', seasoned with the malagueta pepper that Captain Phillips had picked up on the Grain Coast. On three days a week the slaves were also served 'horse-beans boil'd for their dinner and supper, great quantities of which the *African* company do send aboard us for that purpose'. The beans were seen as 'having a binding quality, and consequently good to prevent the flux', which, as Phillips noted, was 'the inveterate distemper that most affects them'.[23] The 'flux' was a catch-all term for intestinal disorders resulting in severe diarrhoea, of which dysentery was the most common.

Dysentery was a deadly scourge on the Middle Passage and once the contagion took hold it was extremely difficult to suppress. So it proved on the *Hannibal*. The faecal stench exuded by the vessel told of a catastrophic outbreak. Dysentery's ravages were exacerbated by the length of time the ship languished in the mid-Atlantic. The *Hannibal* made good initial progress, crossing the line to take advantage of the trade winds that blew strongly to the south of the equator. Between 9 and 15 September 1694 she averaged 120 miles a day. Steering back into the northern hemisphere so as to hit the latitude of Barbados, the *Hannibal* continued at an acceptable pace. Indeed, on 28 September a south-westerly gale propelled the *Hannibal* across 140 miles of ocean. But over the next two days she made just 37 miles, drifting at less than one mile per hour; for the three days after that she was completely becalmed. Being 'perplexed with calms (in which the heats were most intense and unsupportable)', Phillips gave orders that the slaves' allowance of drinking water be cut lest supplies be exhausted before making the West Indies.[24] For those suffering from dysentery, who were already tormented by chronic dehydration, this was a death sentence.

When the epidemic was at its height corpses were tipped in the sea at the rate of a dozen a day. There were no funeral honours, just one final indignity: as soon as they hit the water the dead Africans were torn apart by the escort of sharks that never left the *Hannibal*'s side. The losses were appalling: 320 slaves perished – 45 per cent of those who had been embarked at Whydah. This was an atrocious record. No slave voyage was without death – it was, after all, an exercise in systematic maltreatment – but few voyages were as calamitous as the *Hannibal*'s. Other slave ships that cleared from the Bight of Benin in the seventeenth century lost on average 15 per cent of their human cargo; the *Hannibal* lost three times that. Captain Phillips blamed his victims, not himself. Had he not tried to keep 'their lodgings as clean and sweet as possible'? And had he not taken 'care to give them their messes in due order and season'? The fault lay with the Africans ('a parcel of creatures nastier than swines'), or so their embittered gaoler, who had pinioned them in their own excrement, insisted.

On 4 November 1694, two months and eleven days after leaving São Tomé, the *Hannibal* dropped anchor off Barbados. Her commander's feelings of gloom and self-pity deepened as a reckoning was made with the Royal African Company's local agent. The prisoners who had died represented a loss of £6,650. The lot of the slaver, Phillips concluded, was not a happy one: because of the persistently high mortality of slaves 'our voyages are ruin'd, and we pine and fret ourselves to death, to think that we should undergo so much misery, and take so much pains to so little purpose'.[25] The feelings of the 372 African survivors who hobbled ashore can only be guessed at. They had arrived in England's premier sugar island, where a life of unremitting toil and pitiless discipline awaited them. The captives who had 'a more dreadful apprehension of *Barbadoes* than we do of hell' were to have their fears fully realised.

Thomas Phillips, meanwhile, busied himself with assembling a cargo of plantation produce for the last leg of the Atlantic triangle. He loaded 700 hogsheads of sugar, in addition to some cotton and ginger: high-value tropical commodities that would do something to offset the losses sustained on the *Hannibal*'s slave account. The homeward voyage was delayed for fear of a squadron of French men-of-war operating out of Martinique. It was not until April 1695 that a vast convoy of English vessels, 70-strong, had been assembled. The anticipated French attack did not materialise, but it was no easy cruise for the *Hannibal*'s commander. Thomas Phillips had been afflicted by convulsions for some months. The hearing in his right ear had been badly affected during the cruise along the Guinea coast; now it was totally lost. A fortnight out of Barbados the fits resumed, accompanied by vertigo so severe that Phillips was confined to his cabin for over a month, 'in which time the hearing of my left ear was much impair'd ... and having none to look after me, (my doctor having died of the plague in Barbados) my deafness increas'd daily'. Disability inevitably compromised professional effectiveness and mishaps began to multiply as the *Hannibal* entered English waters. The ship's mate grounded her in Falmouth harbour on 24 May; a week later, the same mate, at the wheel as Phillips lay sick in his cot, 'though obstinacy or folly, refusing to bear up, or tack in time', rammed into another ship off Beachy Head. The *Hannibal* was left 'like a wreck floating in the sea, with her mast and rigging dangling about her ears'.[26] It was the final blow for Phillips. By the time the *Hannibal* had been towed back to Portsmouth for refit his hearing had totally gone. He wrote to Jeffrey Jeffreys to resign his command.

Back in the capital, Thomas Phillips consulted a 'great many applauded physicians' in an attempt to reverse his deafness. A hundred guineas were spent in the endeavour, but fruitlessly. The ex-mariner, his profession now closed to him, retreated to Wales to live 'among my relations in *Brecknock*, my native town, there to spend the rest of my life as easily as I can, under my hard misfortune'.[27] There Phillips died in 1713, twenty years after the *Hannibal* had sailed for Africa. His was a lonely and frustrating old age, no doubt, but there were worse fates. Most of those he had picked out of the trunk at Whydah and condemned to the torments of the Middle Passage were already long dead, the victims of a murderous plantation system.

Thomas Phillips's career as a slaver ended abruptly in 1695; that of Jeffrey Jeffreys did not. He continued as a director of the Royal African Company until 1698, and when the company's monopoly of trade on the Guinea coast was rescinded he lost no time in setting up as an independent trader. He was a partner in nine slaving expeditions that sailed from London between 1698 and 1703, landing nearly 2,300 captives in the Americas: 994 went to Jamaica, 635 to Antigua, 260 to Nevis, 248 to Barbados and 154 to Virginia. Jeffrey Jeffreys remained an active slave merchant until his death, continuing a family tradition initiated by his uncle John in the 1650s.

That the Jeffreys family of Llywel gave rise to a Welsh slaving mini-dynasty says nothing specific about the relationship between Wales and Atlantic slavery, however. The role of Jeffrey Jeffreys, his uncle and his brother in shipping thousands of enslaved Africans over a period of more than fifty years reveals that slave trading was a colossal international enterprise that required large amounts of capital, drawn from large numbers of investors. Inevitably, some were Welsh, but most were not. Indeed, capital-poor upland Wales was an unlikely point of origin for major slave merchants. The substantial sums that successive members of the Jeffreys family directed into the Guinea trade, it should be remembered, had been accumulated in London, not Llywel. They were Welsh, but their Welshness had no special bearing on their slaving activities.

By the same token, sizeable numbers of Welsh seamen must have participated in slave voyages during the long decades in which British merchants dominated the trade. '*Thomas Cronow*, an honest stout *Welshman*', was one of those who died of their wounds after the *Hannibal*'s battle with the *Louis* in 1693.[1] The proximity of Bristol and Liverpool must have tempted many others to follow in his wake. Two brothers, Evan and William William, from Michaelston-super-Ely in the Vale of Glamorgan, were among those who did so. Tired of village life ('being young lads that gave themselves to a riotous sort of life', as a local diarist noted sourly), they signed on a Bristol slave ship in March 1768.[2] They had no more luck than Thomas Cronow: both died in the tropics. The presence of Welsh sailors did not lend Atlantic slavery a distinctively Welsh flavour, however. Crewmen from coastal Wales, like Welsh-built ships, were a tiny minority; their involvement was an incidental, not a structural feature of the trade.

Yet there were ways in which Wales did become structurally embedded in Atlantic slavery. Captain Thomas Phillips pointed to one of these when discussing the variety of trade goods needed on the Guinea coast. At some places particular sorts of textiles were required, at others iron bars; but at Whydah the goods that were in most demand – aside from the ubiquitous cowries – were brass pans, 'very large, thin and flat', known as 'neptunes'.

European brass and copper wares had already been traded in this way for two centuries when Captain Phillips made his observation. Brass pans were employed for a wide variety of purposes: industrial (the evaporation of salt, say), domestic (the washing of the body) and votive (by being incorporated into shrines). Manillas of brass and copper served both as personal decoration and as currency. The men of the Windward Coast, an English naval surgeon of the 1730s observed, were rarely seen without 'Manilla's, about their Wrists and Ancles, of Brass, Copper, Pewter, or Ivory'.[3] The Portuguese had been bartering brass manillas on the Gold Coast as early as the 1470s and by the early sixteenth century huge quantities of brass and copper were being shipped south. No fewer than 216,700 manillas and 9,000 brass and copper basins were traded for gold at Elmina in a single 25-month period between 1529 and 1531. Having no copper industry of their own, the Portuguese imported cuprous goods from Flanders. The same manufacturing networks were to serve the Dutch with equal facility during their period of dominance in the Guinea trade. The products of historic brass-making centres like Dinant, Liège, Aachen and Stolberg flowed naturally towards the Dutch Republic. When the English began their systematic entry into the slave trade in the 1660s and 1670s they accessed the same supply chains. The Royal African Company obtained its brass wares via Rotterdam. By the 1690s, however, alternative sources of supply were beginning to emerge, alternatives that could be traced to Wales.

Brass is an alloy of copper and zinc, with copper as the principal constituent. In the fifteenth and sixteenth centuries Europe's principal copper-producing centres were in the German lands: the Tyrol and Saxony. By the seventeenth century, however, the great days of the Saxon and Tyrolean mining districts were in the past. Exports from Sweden, which shot upward from the 1620s, made good the shortfall. Yet Swedish copper proved a short-lived substitute. In 1687 the enormous mine at Falun, the main source of supply for baroque Europe, suffered a catastrophic cave-in that suspended production completely for a number of years and whose ill effects were never fully overcome. New sources of supply were urgently needed if north European brass manufacture was to remain buoyant.

Happily, it was just at this moment that ore lodes were being opened up in Cornwall as tin miners, who had been active in the far west of England throughout the early modern period, drove their workings deeper underground and began to encounter appreciable cuprous deposits mixed in with the veins of tin. The presence of copper galvanised mining speculators and led to a rush of investment in Cornwall. But for ore extraction to flourish there had to be fuel with which to smelt it. In the seventeenth century that meant charcoal because a way of using mineral coal without imparting sulphurous impurities into the metallic copper had yet to be devised. In Sweden, with its abundant forests, this was not a difficulty. In wood-depleted Cornwall it was an acute problem, hence the efforts made by a variety of entrepreneurs in the late seventeenth century to employ mineral fuel in the smelting of copper. One of the pioneers in this field was a versatile businessman named William Dockwra (c.1635–1716), whose past accomplishments included interloping on the Royal African Company. Dockwra's technical adjutant – the really key figure in all of this – was John Coster (1647–1718), whose descendants were to be of critical importance for the development of a Welsh copper industry.

With Dockwra's backing, Coster established a coal-fired smelting works at Redbrook in the lower Wye valley in 1689 and quickly established the viability of his new methods. It was a revolutionary development. In the course of the next century native ores, freed from the constraints imposed by vegetable fuel, were to propel the British – or as it increasingly became, Welsh – copper industry from the European margins to global dominance. A second plant was promptly erected at Redbrook by a rival group of capitalists in 1692, but the most visible effect of Coster's breakthrough was a sprouting of copper and brass production facilities in and around Bristol. There was a compelling spatial logic at work: locally smelted copper could now be combined with calamine (zinc carbonate) brought in from the Mendip hills to the south of the city, so the Avon valley was ideally placed for the crucibles and battery hammers of brass makers.

Bristol remained an important organisational centre for the copper and brass trades throughout the eighteenth century, but copper production facilities soon started to slip westward into Wales. Sir Humphry Mackworth (1657–1727), a tireless gentleman-entrepreneur in west Glamorgan, had a smelting plant up and running on his coal-bearing estate in Neath in the mid-1690s and in 1713, as the head of a joint-stock company called the Mineral Manufacturers of Neath, he extended into brass making. The migration of the copper industry into Wales is readily explained. Seaborne Cornish ores could be brought directly to the abundant, outcropping coal of the Swansea-Neath district. (As several tons of coal was burnt in smelting one ton of ore it was rational to ship the ore to coal deposits rather than ship coal to Cornwall.) Bristol's industrialists soon took note.

A Bristol man, Dr John Lane, had been one of those involved in the Mineral Manufacturers of Neath. In 1717 he moved on to build the first dedicated copper smelting plant in the Swansea valley: a massive, streamlined works at Llangyfelach. John Coster's sons, who had built up extensive mining interests in Cornwall and north Devon, followed suit, shifting their smelting operations from Bristol to south Wales. They took over premises at Melincryddan in the Neath valley c.1730, then a huge, purpose-built works at White Rock in the Swansea valley in the late 1730s. The Coster family are worthy of special note, not just because they embody copper's shift to coal technology and to Wales at the turn of the eighteenth century, but because they exemplify Welsh copper's intimate links with the slave trade of Bristol.

There was an eerie symmetry between the smelting of copper in south Wales and Bristol slaving. The city's 'golden' age as a slave port extended from the 1710s to the 1740s. It was within just this time-frame that Swansea emerged as the foremost centre of copper smelting in Europe. It was no accident that the two should rise in tandem. Bristol merchants had been quick to respond to the revocation in 1698 of the Royal African Company's monopoly of trade on the Guinea Coast. These Bristol men were soon making incursions into the Bight of Biafra, well to the east of the trading areas that had been exploited by the London-based company in the late seventeenth century. The Bight was the new frontier of British slaving, and its traders were interested in particular types of trade goods – metallic ones. As Thomas Phillips had explained to his readers, different parts of the coast served different hinterlands, and each of these had particular demands to make on the international market. If Europeans were to procure slaves they had to attend closely to the shifting contours of African demand, whether that demand was for Indian-made cottons or woollens woven in Wales. Each stretch of the coast had its peculiarities, and it so happened that along the Bight of Biafra copper rods were indispensable as a medium of exchange. Sometimes they circulated in the form in which they arrived from Europe; at other times the rods would be beaten out by African smiths and woven into cables.

It was this appetite for copper and copper-based wares that drew copper masters like the Costers into the Guinea trade. Thomas Coster (1684–1739), the head of the family in the 1720s and 1730s, was an enthusiastic slaver. He was part-owner of the 85-ton *Amoretta*, purpose-built in New England in 1726 to carry captive Africans from the Bight of Biafra. Coster was no casual member of Bristol's slaving community. On the contrary, his partners in the *Amoretta* included Joseph Iles and Isaac Hobhouse, two of the city's most eminent slave merchants. And the *Amoretta* was no isolated experiment. In the mid-1730s, as the Costers prepared to launch the White Rock smelting works, they also ploughed capital into slaving expeditions. Thomas Coster was part-owner of the *Mary*, launched at Bristol in 1735 and promptly set to work running slaves to Jamaica. And in 1737 he joined once more with Iles and Hobhouse to fit out the *Squirrel*, a new-built colonial vessel that joined the *Amoretta* in carrying slaves to the Carolina Lowcountry, British North America's most brutal slave society, then undergoing a massive boom as rice cultivation was extended through the coastal marshes and inland swamps. Between 1732 and 1739 the *Amoretta* made seven trips to South Carolina at Thomas Coster's behest, landing 1,539 Africans at Charles Town. The Bristol merchant and Welsh copper master lost his investment in a further 389 unfortunates. They perished before the *Amoretta* made landfall. As for those who sailed on the *Squirrel* and the *Mary*, no information on their numbers or fate has survived.

The Costers were not alone in embracing both copper and slavery. When the Llangyfelach partners shipped their products to Bristol they were consigned to James Laroche. Laroche features in the authoritative study of the Swansea copper industry as the Bristol agent of the Llangyfelach partnership.[1] Such is the view from Swansea; the perspective from Bristol is rather different. There, James Laroche looms large as the city's mightiest slave merchant in the 1730s and 1740s. In 1738, a busy year in the Atlantic slave trade, James Laroche & Co fitted out no fewer than five slaving expeditions, carrying manacled Africans to Jamaica, St Kitts and South Carolina. Laroche condemned 1,355 to the Middle Passage in this single year, one in five of whom did not survive the process. What part of their purchase price was paid with copper rods and brass wares remains unknown. Indeed, the slave ports to which Laroche & Co despatched cargoes are not recorded – with one exception. The *Levant*, a vessel of 200 tons, left Bristol to pick up a cargo of captives at Bonny, an emergent trading centre in the Cross River delta, on one of the braided waterways that stretched inland from the Bight of Biafra, where copper rods had long been used as a currency. It would have been remarkable if James Laroche had not had Swansea copper stowed aboard the *Levant*.

From the very beginning Welsh copper and brass makers paid close attention to African wants. The proprietors of the Llangyfelach works complemented the smelting plant built in 1717 with battery works at which pans and kettles could be manufactured. The earliest known print of the Costers' White Rock works dates from 1744. It identifies one of the structures as the 'Manilla House' where those articles, which had no sale other than in African slave marts, were presumably cast. The same concern for satisfying African consumers was shown in Flintshire, the other great centre of copper and brass manufacture in Wales, where the Holywell stream, which tumbled down into the Dee, powered a succession of battery hammers and mills for the 'great copper-companies, those *behemoths* of commerce'.[2] The Swedish traveller Reinhold Angerstein, who stopped at the Greenfield works on Deeside in the early 1750s, watched copper rods being prepared. The rods were drawn out under a trip hammer. Angerstein was a little surprised to see the work done in this way. 'The production would take much less time', he wrote, 'if the rods were drawn through holes in an iron plate, as is done with heavy brass wire, but I was told that this way of processing would not give the copper the same degree of ductility.' And ductility was an essential quality because, Angerstein added, the 'Negroes in Guinea use the rods as ornaments and wind them around arms and legs'. Indeed, these lengths of copper had a simple and expressive trade name: 'Negroes'.[3]

A generation after Angerstein's visit the works that lined the banks of the Holywell were under the control of Thomas Williams (1737–1802), an Anglesey solicitor who had 'with unparalleled speed, covered the lower part of the stream, or that next to the sea, with buildings stupendous in expence, extent, and ingenuity of contrivance'.[4] As this awed description suggests, Williams was an out-of-the-ordinary character. He had first become involved in the copper trade in a legal capacity, by acting for a landowner upon whose Parys Mountain estate rich reserves of copper ore were discovered in the 1760s. He was no mere scrivener, however; Thomas Williams was soon revealed as a man of boundless commercial ambition and razor-like acumen. He became the driving force behind the Parys Mine Company in the 1770s and, after amalgamation with a rival mining concern in the 1780s, he had the entire ore output of Anglesey at his disposal. Enormous quantities were extracted from Parys Mountain, which was clawed apart by pick and by powder. It was a spectacle that stunned a succession of visitors.

> I found myself standing on the verge of a vast and tremendous chasm . . . and the prospect was dreadful. The number of caverns at different heights along the sides; the broken and irregular masses of rock which everywhere present themselves; the multitudes of men at work in different parts, and apparently in the most perilous of situations; the motion of the Whimsies [winding engines], and the raising and lowering of the buckets, to draw out the ores and the rubbish; the noise of picking the ore from rock, and of hammering the wadding, when it was about to be blasted, with, at intervals, the roar of the blasts in distant parts of the mine, altogether excited the most sublime ideas, intermixt, however, with sensations of terror.[5]

Parys Mountain ore was not as rich as its deep-mined Cornish counterpart, but it was obtainable by open-cast methods, allowing Williams to outmanoeuvre his rivals in the far southwest. The flow of cut-price ore onto the market brought its own difficulties, of course. It gave the whip hand to the smelters. The Cornish ore producers responded to the fall in the market value by establishing a cartel to set prices: the Cornish Metal Company. Williams was perfectly happy for the power of the smelters to be curbed – provided it was on his terms. He decided to force Cornwall's mine adventurers into an all-embracing national monopoly that was unequivocally under his direction. Many doubted whether the notoriously fractious Cornishmen could be brought into line. In the event, though, they were driven 'like sheep'. Thomas Williams, together with his associate John Wilkinson, another ferociously strong-willed industrialist, confronted the Cornish mine owners head on at a public meeting in Truro in 1785. Matthew Boulton, the Birmingham manufacturer who was also in on the plan, was delighted with the results of Williams and Wilkinson's rough-house approach: 'The Cornishmen would not have submitted to have been kicked and piss'd upon by me as they have been by them.'[6] Williams, he wrote, had 'risen very high in my estimation'.

With the price of ore in Britain now being dictated from Anglesey, Thomas Williams set about acquiring works at which the ore he controlled could be refined and readied for market. He had smelting furnaces at two locations in Lancashire and three around Swansea, now firmly established as the centre of the British copper industry: Upper Bank and Middle Bank, just upstream from the old White Rock works of the Costers, and Penclawdd, to the west of the town. The Flintshire mills at Greenfield and Holywell completed one of the most commanding industrial complexes of the age. Slavery lay at the root of it all – or so Thomas Williams maintained. Petitioning the House of Lords in 1788, when the first moves to regulate the slave trade were afoot, the 'Copper King' claimed that it had been the demand for copper in Africa that had induced him and his Parys Mountain associates to lay out £70,000 on facilities at Holywell, Penclawdd and Temple Mills. The articles they manufactured were 'entirely for the African market and not saleable for any other'.[7] Had it not been for manillas, neptunes and Guinea kettles, he suggested, Parys Mountain would have lain undisturbed and the Holywell district would not have been disfigured by the 'tremendous volumes of thick black smoke' that issued from the 'vast square chimnies' of his different works.[8]

This was special pleading. The copper and brass trades were exceptionally export orientated, with perhaps 40 per cent of output being shipped overseas, but Africa was not the only market, nor even the largest. Asia absorbed very substantial volumes of refined copper in the late eighteenth century. Thomas Williams knew this well, having captured the highly lucrative East India Company contract not long previously, but as many of his business rivals could attest, the Anglesey man was not over scrupulous about the truth. The Guinea trade was threatened by meddling legislators, so Williams sprang to its defence with a shrill and not wholly truthful insistence on its centrality to his copper business. If this required a tactical downplaying of the extent of copper shipments on East Indiamen, so be it. Yet there is some justice in seeing the export to Asia as an *indirect* contribution to the slave commerce of the Atlantic. The copper shipped to India – most of it smelted in the Swansea and Neath valleys, naturally – was exchanged for a range of local commodities amongst which cottons figured prominently: chintzes, calicos, muslins, nicanees and photaes. These were the very textiles that the East India Company sold in such large volume to slavers for re-export to Africa.

It should also be said that much of the Welsh-smelted copper that was, on the face of things, consumed domestically facilitated the Guinea trade. The sharp upturn in the consumption of copper by the Royal Navy and Britain's merchant fleet after the 1760s provides the most notable example. Vessels that plied trop-ical waters suffered from the relentless attack of wood-boring marine creatures. One species of mollusc, *teredo navalis*, was ruinously persistent in this respect. Its depredations had such serious effects on vessels' seaworthiness that they were forced into frequent and lengthy stays in port to have their hulls careened, which diminished the operational effectiveness of His Majesty's ships and cut into the profit margins of commercial ship owners. The ships that were most affected were, of course, those that sailed to the warmer latitudes: that is, slave ships, merchantmen engaged in the shipping of sugar and other slave-produced commodities, and that part of the Royal Navy charged with protecting Britain's super-lucrative West Indian commerce. A method of shielding timber hulls from the attentions of *teredo navalis* was therefore keenly sought out.

Copper sheathing was trialled by the Navy Board in the 1760s. The advantages were clear enough. Pestiferous molluscs could get no purchase on a sleek metallic surface. Hulls remained cleaner and unholed, resulting in greater speed and superior manoeuvrability, and less time was spent in dock. From the point of view of the British state, having ships 'copper-bottomed' had much to recommend it. It made use of a metal that was now produced domestically in large quantities and exploited advances in rolling technology that rival maritime powers could not easily match. Welsh copper manufacturers were the beneficiaries of the new policy. The contractors for sheet copper in 1780, for example, were two firms in the Neath valley (the Gnoll Company and the Mines Royal Company) and the Macclesfield Company, which at that time had a part-interest in the ore of Parys Mountain and operated a processing mill in Flintshire.

The one difficulty with copper sheathing lay in fastening the sheets to the wooden hull. The iron bolts that were used at first corroded very rapidly, the victims of a galvanic reaction with the copper and salt water with which they necessarily came into contact. The sheathing came adrift with equal rapidity. So serious was the problem that the Navy Board was on the verge of abandoning the coppering of ships in the early 1780s. Using copper bolts to fix on the sheets would have avoided the damaging chemical effervescence, but copper has none of the natural hardness of iron. A solution was engineered by Thomas Williams, who sponsored experiments in the cold-rolling of copper that produced bolts of the necessary resilience. By 1784 the Anglesey man had the contract for supplying the Royal Navy; he was turning out 40,000 hardened copper bolts weekly at the Holywell works. Welsh copper was, quite literally, holding together the naval force that guaranteed security for slave traders and slaveholders in Britain's Atlantic empire.

The copper industry was revolutionised in the eighteenth century – revolutionised from Wales. In 1690 global output of smelted copper stood at just 2,400 tons, none of it Welsh. By 1800 production worldwide was 17,200 tons, of which 41 per cent was smelted in Wales. This astonishing phase of expansion, spearheaded by Welsh copper producers, paved the way for a re-ordering of international trade in the metal and the wares made from it. Britain became the source of the best part of the world's traded copper. As can be imagined, Africa figured largely in this. British exports of brass and copper to Africa in the eighteenth century showed two characteristics. The first was phenomenal growth. The combined export of brass and copper amounted to just 324 tons between 1701 and 1710, but in the 1730s, as the Welsh smelting sector gathered strength, exports topped 1,000 tons, and in the 1780s, when the British slave trade was at its apogee, exports exceeded 3,000 tons. The second characteristic to be noted is the plummeting of re-exports. Of the 324 tons exported in the first decade of the eighteenth century, 200 tons (67 per cent) was actually of foreign origin: Swedish copper and brassware brought in from Holland. In the 1730s such re-exports had shrunk to 37 per cent of the total export, and by the 1780s they had disappeared completely. Coal-based smelting and processing on the Welsh model had triumphed, and by triumphing allowed British slave traders to inundate African markets with home-produced copper and brass goods.

But there was one further overseas market, the largest of all, which has yet to be mentioned. This took nearly half of copper exports, wrought and unwrought, on the eve of the American Revolution: the West Indies. Here again, copper sales were linked to slavery. The business of plantations in the West Indies was the making of sugar and distilling of rum. This was done on an industrial scale, using methods that that required huge copper vessels. The sap obtained from crushed sugar cane was collected in copper pans called clarifiers. 'Of these, there are commonly three; and their dimensions are generally determined by the power of supplying them with liquor.' Some were quite enormous, with capacities ranging up to 1,000 gallons. A suite of these could boil off thirty hogsheads of sugar weekly during the harvest. Admittedly, they were only to be found on uncommonly large plantations. More usual, reported one eighteenth-century authority, were estates 'that make on a medium during crop-time, from fifteen to twenty hogsheads of sugar a week. On such estates, three clarifiers of three or four hundred gallons each are sufficient.'[9] The copper utensils needed for distilling rum were no less impressive. 'The still-houses on the sugar-plantations in the British West Indies, vary greatly in point of size and expence, according to the fancy of the proprietor, or the magnitude of the property', it was reported, with the largest stills holding between 'one to three thousand gallons of liquor'. Once again, such colossi were not the norm, but the standard equipment was large enough: 'two copper stills, the one of one thousand two hundred, and the other of six hundred gallons' were required.[10]

The explosive growth of the market for clarifiers and stills over the course of the eighteenth century is brought starkly to the fore by statistics from Jamaica. The island, which overtook Barbados as a sugar exporter in the first years of the eighteenth century, had 400 plantations at work in 1730, producing 25,000 hogsheads of sugar, all of it intended for export. By 1754 sugar exports stood at 40,000 hogsheads and by 1768 at over 68,000 hogsheads – a rise of 172 per cent in little more than a generation. A huge quantity of Welsh copper stood behind these spiralling figures. The sugar islands – slave islands – formed one of the most dynamic growth points in the British world. Labour, land and capital were exploited with unparalleled intensity. Export commodities were pumped out at a terrific rate; industrial supplies and provisions for the enslaved were sucked in with matching speed. Welsh copper, rolled out and riveted into a variety of forms, was one contribution to this mighty engine; it was not the only one that Wales had to make.

By 1700 the English empire in the western Atlantic – a British empire after the union of 1707 with Scotland – curved along an arc that stretched from the Grand Banks of Newfoundland to the Caribbean. The most productive and the most cherished parts of this empire lay in the south. The 'English Shore' of Newfoundland hosted a valuable seasonal fishery, but few people actually lived year-round on that bleak, foggy coast. New England, scarcely more hospitable in winter, had a large settled population but the contribution of the colony's farmers to Atlantic commerce was not pronounced. They were the descendants of the religious fanatics who had left England in the Great Migration of the 1630s. Their forebears had gone to the New World to escape the Old, not to commune with it further, and New Englanders retained a certain wariness.

The commercial empire was based upon two great staples, sugar from the West Indies and tobacco from Virginia, both of which boomed in the middle decades of the seventeenth century. Barbados was the first English island to be struck by the 'sugar revolution'. Those who had colonised the island in the 1620s and 1630s had been socially mixed: a yeomanry supported by indentured white servants, experimenting with a variety of crops, some for subsistence, some for export, on a motley patchwork of farms. By the 1680s, however, the social structure had been transformed. It was now polarised between a small, super-wealthy planter elite and a mass of enslaved Africans who were kept in check by unremitting terror. The economy was now wholly export driven. The sugar revolution had brought about 'a swift shift from diversified agriculture to sugar monoculture, from production on small farms to large plantations, from free labour to slave labour, from sparse to dense settlement, [and] from white to black populations'.[1] The transition was repeated in England's other islands in the Lesser Antilles (Nevis, St Kitts, Montserrat and Antigua) in short order. In the 1670s it seized Jamaica, transforming the island in little more than a generation from a privateering base with no more than desultory agriculture to England's richest sugar colony.

The spread of sugar through the Caribbean had been slave-dependent from the outset. Things were different with tobacco. During the early decades of commercial cultivation along the Chesapeake – from the 1620s to the 1670s – tobacco was cultivated by white farmers with the assistance of indentured labourers. These servants were overwhelmingly of English or Welsh descent: young men and women who were without resource or prospect in the economically sombre years of the mid-seventeenth century. Bereft of hope at home, they signed a contract – an indenture – with a merchant or ship's master in London or Bristol, pledging their labour for a period of years in return for their passage to the New World. When their ship dropped anchor in the Chesapeake, the captain would auction off his passengers' indentures. They would be bought by planters who were eager for labour. An indenture specified the period over which a servant would have to toil (usually between four and seven years) and set out the basic conditions of service: that a servant would be fed, housed and clothed adequately, and that he or she would receive a small lump sum ('freedom dues') when their term was served.

Work in the tobacco fields was arduous, the diet sometimes meagre and masters often tyrannical, but indentured servants did enjoy judicial freedom and legal protection. Where masters were excessively abusive the servant could appeal to a magistrate with some hope of redress. The terms of their servitude were closely defined and of limited duration. The lot of slaves was vastly different. The most bestial violence could be used against them, they went clothed or naked at their master's whim and their labour was without limit. Only death brought release, and even then slaves knew that their servile status was heritable and that their offspring would also be the property of their master. It was this potential for unconfined, perpetual exploitation that made slavery increasingly attractive to Virginia's tobacco planters. Indentured servants were notoriously protective of their legal rights and resistant to their masters' authority. Slaves could be terrorised without qualm. Besides, the supply of servants was tightening. The late seventeenth century saw slackening population growth and a concomitant rise in living standards in England and Wales. Economic opportunity at home made young men and women less willing to sail for the Chesapeake. So it was that between the 1680s and the 1720s Virginia, whose fields had once been worked largely by white servants, swung over to being a colony based upon the labour of enslaved Africans.

Before the 1680s there was no direct slave trade from Africa to Virginia. Slaves entered the colony indirectly, sold on via the sugar islands to the south. The numbers were small, so that there were no more than 3,000 captive labourers present in 1680, accounting for just 7 per cent of the population. By 1720 though, the number of slaves had leapt to over 26,000; they now made up 30 per cent of the total population. A generation later, their numbers had bounded up once more to

107,000, equivalent to 46 per cent of the total. A still more abrupt transformation was underway in the other major growth-point in early eighteenth-century British North America: South Carolina. For the best part of a generation after the colony's foundation in 1670 slaves made up a minor part of the population. Cattle ranching, forestry and the trade in deerskins were the principal economic activities. By 1700, however, the cultivation of rice was extending rapidly through the swampy Carolina Lowcountry. This required a massive injection of labour, for rice needed constant attention whilst in the field and extensive processing once harvested. These were gruelling tasks, to be performed in conditions of oppressive heat and humidity. Field labourers had to stand 'ancle, and even mid-leg deep in water ... exposed all the while to a burning sun, which makes the very air they breathe hotter than the human blood; these poor wretches are then in a furnace of stinking putrid effluvia'.[2] Nothing but coercion would be able to mobilise the numbers required, hence the resort to large-scale slavery. In 1700 free white settlers were still a majority in the province, but by 1720 black people made up 70 per cent of a much expanded population. Carolina had become the most 'African' spot in British North America, resembling more closely in its demography and the ferocity of its labour code the sugar islands to the south than the other mainland colonies, even Virginia.

The transformation of South Carolina from a sparsely settled frontier zone to a plantation colony between 1690 and 1720 completed the 'slave belt' that accounted for the most populous and economically potent parts of Britain's Atlantic empire. Virginia, the Lowcountry and the sugar islands were all export focused, producing for far distant markets and using major concentrations of enslaved workers. The plantations – or labour camps – were highly specialised: they were dedicated to the growing and processing of a single export commodity, and they produced very little else. Everything else, starting with the labour force, was imported. That included the processing equipment – such as copper clarifiers and stills in the case of sugar plantations – and the 'necessaries' needed to sustain the labour force: food and clothing. Because the islands and coastal strips that made up the slave empire were so densely populated they drew in essential supplies with enormous centripetal force. Rapidly growing slave numbers meant escalating demand, which stimulated suppliers right around the Atlantic world.

The need for protein had New England merchants shipping vast quantities of salt cod from the Grand Banks of Newfoundland to the Caribbean; their counterparts in Glasgow sent barrelled herring. Irish beef satisfied the same calorific requirement. In the middle of the eighteenth century between 50,000 and 80,000 cattle were slaughtered in Cork every year. The beasts that were disassembled, salted and packed in this high-throughput operation were largely destined for the New World where their flesh was to be gnawed on by slaves. Slaves had to be clothed as well as fed; that too involved the transportation of 'necessaries' across thousands of miles. The fabric that most captives wore next to their skin was 'oznabrigs', a cheap linen so called because it originated in Osnabrück in northern Germany or, at least, had once. By the eighteenth century linens made in the style of Osnabrück had become a generic good, allowing planters to buy 'oznabrigs' manufactured in the west of Scotland or northern England specifically for slave use. Slaves might also be issued with knee-length hose, often knitted in Scotland. Francis Jerdone, a storekeeper in Tidewater Virginia, sold a variety of Scottish-made goods to local tobacco planters in the 1740s and 1750s: 'Aberdeen Stockings' and 'Kilmarnock hose' were among them.[3] But the major ingredient in slave costume was provided by coarse woollens, and these, more often than not, were from Wales.

Slaves in the New World would seldom have known of Wales, but they knew the adjective Welsh, for 'Welsh cotton' or 'Welsh plains' made up the basic uniform of the enslaved. When Solomon, a nineteen-year-old slave, ran away from his master in Northumberland County, Virginia, in February 1767 he was wearing 'a WELSH Cotton Jacket ... [and] a Pair of Country Cloth Breeches'. That, at least, was the claim of his master when he issued a reward notice in the *Maryland Gazette* appealing for the capture and return of his property.[1] As was usual in such advertisements, the clothing and distinguishing marks of the fugitive were described. It was taken for granted that the readers of the *Maryland Gazette* would know what 'a WELSH Cotton Jacket' looked like.

The 'cotton' was, in fact, a woollen fabric, one whose nap had been teased upwards or 'cottoned'. It was a product of midland Wales, of a band that stretched across Montgomeryshire and Merionethshire – although Francis Jerdone, who sold substantial quantities of Welsh woollens from his store at Yorktown, also retailed 'Brecknockshire plains' and 'Brecknockshire Cottons'.[2] Woollen textiles were, of course, a historic product of Wales. In the late middle ages their making had been centred upon urban nodes in the south: Carmarthen, Pembroke, Monmouth. During the sixteenth and seventeenth centuries, however, woollen manufacturing decamped to upland pastoral districts where impoverished peasant households sought a way of boosting their incomes. The production of low-quality textiles was a characteristic response. The carding of raw wool and the spinning of yarn could be done in the slack periods that broke up the agricultural routine of the wet uplands. Looms could be accommodated in lean-to additions to farmhouses and cottages. The proliferation of fulling mills along mountain streams and cascades in Montgomeryshire and Merionethshire in the sixteenth and seventeenth centuries is an index of the industry's growth. It is one of the few indices available, for this widely dispersed domestic trade otherwise left few traces in the form of guilds or cloth halls.

Fulling (the battering of the freshly woven fabric whilst wet to increase and even out the tension between warp and weft) was the only finishing operation carried out locally. High-value, high-skill processes such as shearing (the trimming of the raised nap to give a consistently smooth surface to the cloth) were carried out at Shrewsbury, where the powerful Drapers Company exerted a tight grip on the marketing of mid-Wales textiles. The commercial monopoly exercised by Shrewsbury's drapers and later by other English agents was to ensure that the profits of what became a very substantial export trade percolated back to farmsteads and hamlets in Montgomeryshire and Merionethshire slowly and imperfectly. The final product was exported via London, where a 'Welch Hall' was maintained for factors' convenience, usually to France.[3] There was, however, in the later seventeenth century a switch in the nature of the product and its destination. Welsh producers concentrated more on lighter flannels and plains rather than heavy broadcloth, and these were intended for Atlantic markets.

Although the slave societies of the New World were to provide the major market for Welsh 'cottons' and 'plains' (the latter, as the name suggests, a fabric that had not been subjected to any kind of elaborate finish), at the end of the seventeenth century Welsh-made woollens also appeared in African slave marts. The Royal African Company bought substantial quantities for export to the Gold Coast. Early in November 1716, for example, the company placed two major orders with the London merchant Samuel Monck for forty 'halfe plains' – a half-plain being a length of fabric that stretched for about eighty yards – at twelve pence per yard and a further thirty half-plains at fourteen pence. That amounted to 5,483 yards. Monck was back before the Committee of Goods, which handled the company's procurement, four days later. This time he contracted for an additional 806 yards. Two further consignments were agreed upon eleven days after that. In all, Monck agreed to deliver over 8,600 yards of Welsh plains – or more than five and half miles.[4]

The cloth that Samuel Monck delivered was 'white'. It was yet to be dyed. The Royal African Company took care of that itself, or rather it put the cloth out to be dyed and packed by specialist subcontractors in London. Once vibrantly coloured, the fabric was brought back before the Committee of Goods to be inspected. Enormous care was taken because colour was the all-important selling point on the African coast. The price of 'Welch plaines' at the company's trading lodge at Sekondi varied according to shade: in June 1683 blues fetched ten 'angels' (equivalent to one-sixteenth of an ounce of gold), greens were sold at nine angels and reds at eight. The company's newly installed agent soon discovered, however, that blue plains were over valued. 'I am in want of green Welch plaines', he told his superiors at Cape Coast Castle in October 1683, 'blew Welch plaines are noe commodity here, I have a parcell of them but [they] will not sell'.[5] Yet at Dixcove, a little to the west, blue Welsh plains were indispensable. The local headmen demanded them as 'dashes' – *douceurs* – before they would allow trading to begin: 'The Cabbosheers expect all to have cloths of blue Welsh plaines', it was reported in 1692.[6] At Anashan, further down the Gold Coast, sweeteners were also expected in the form of Welsh plains, but this time green: 'The Cabbosheers of this place demand for their Christmass dashees . . . two green Welch plains and eight gallons brandy.'[7]

Neither the wool nor the workmanship in these woollens was of superlative quality. Indeed, the fabric was often so disregarded that African buyers unravelled the wool to have it re-woven in a style more to their liking. The Royal African Company's man at Appa in modern-day Nigeria anticipated a brisk sale of Welsh plains amongst the people of his district 'by reasons they make all their rich cloathes of them'. The local ruler, he related, 'gave me a cloath made of Welch plaine which is very handsome'. More sales could be expected if sufficient care was taken with 'the severall sorts of colours, red, green, yellow, blew, purple and orange'.[8]

This was a niche market, however. The value of the Royal African Company's annual export of Welsh plains averaged just £339 in the five years between 1690 and 1694 (the time of the *Hannibal*'s voyage to Guinea). Over the same period the company's export of sayes, a fabric characteristic of East Anglia, averaged £1,815 and that of perpetuanas, a hard-wearing worsted usually made in Devon, £6,480.[9] That remained the case in the new century. At Cape Coast Castle 200 pieces of blue Welsh plains were kept as a standard item of stock in the first decade of the eighteenth century; by way of contrast, 10,000 pieces of blue 'perpet', which together with Barbadian rum was deemed essential for trade on the Gold Coast at that time, were retained as policy.[10] The boom market for Welsh plains lay elsewhere, in the rocketing slave populations of the Caribbean and British North America. Statistics indicating the growth of this literally captive market require little elaboration. In 1696 there were already 87,000 people of African birth or descent in the British sugar islands. By 1748 the slave population had reached 255,000; by 1815 it topped 743,000.[11] The rise in numbers in the mainland colonies was equally vertiginous. There were fewer than 7,000 enslaved black people in 1680, most of them in the Chesapeake, but by 1750 their numbers exceeded 240,000, and a further surge took the total to 455,000 on the eve of the Revolution.[12]

'You know', a Georgia planter told his London supplier in 1764, 'that 5 yds of Plains usually makes a mans jacket & Breeches or a womans gown'.[13] It was also understood that a new set of clothes would be required every autumn, as a year's labour would reduce the old suit to rags. If so, the market for Welsh woollens was potentially immense. Not only did slave populations grow massively in absolute terms, there was almost certainly a growth in the per capita consumption of textiles. The earliest phases of the plantation system saw the workforce exploited in the crudest ways. The field gangs were worked to the limits of human endurance and the bare minimum was spent on their sustenance. They were worked to death, pure and simple. By the last decades of the eighteenth century, however, competitive pressures led planters (or more usually their managers) to consider exploitation in a more sophisticated fashion. Many planters came to believe that measures of 'amelioration' could enhance the productivity of their slaves. Allowing slaves time to cultivate garden plots of their own, for example, would add variety to their diet and do something to extend their longevity. Improving the medical care extended to pregnant women and new mothers would help reduce the all-too-common miscarriages and infant deaths that prevented the populations of the labour camps reproducing themselves. By the same token, improvements to the dress of the enslaved could have positive and profitable results for the planters. Spending next to nothing on clothing, many managers argued, was a false economy. Resentment at a master's niggardliness could lead to go-slows and sabotage. A Virginia planter thought a neighbour erred in keeping his slaves as 'a kind of Adamites, very scantily supplied with clothes'. The shivering bondsmen and women took their revenge by making 'but indifferent crops, so that he gets nothing by his injustice but the scandal of it'.[14] Slaves who went naked were also vulnerable to disease. 'I assure you Sir', a plantation manager on Nevis told his master, 'that they [the slaves] suffered very much without them [clothes], and the Work that they loose [sic], by Sickness Occasioned from Severe Colds for want of cloaths amounts to a greater loss than the price of the Cloaths'.[15] Welsh plains provided a modestly priced solution to the problem. The whole purpose of Welsh woollens, one observer went so far as to state in the 1770s, was 'covering the poor Negroes in the West Indies'.[16]

There were rival products – like 'Kendall cottons' from the Lake District, a district as inhospitable and impoverished as mid-Wales, or 'penistones' from moorland Yorkshire – but Wales appears to have been the major source of what contemporaries called Negro Cloth. 'Good Welch cotton seems upon the whole to answer best', the Virginia slave holder William Lee announced; others were 'light and insufficient'.[17] When Elias Ball, an exiled American loyalist, investigated the source of the Negro Cloth in which the slaves of his native South Carolina were clad he discovered that 'the great Markett for that article ... is at Shroesberry [sic] the Capital of Shropshire'.[18] Unlike the 'Welch cotton' that the Royal African Company shipped to Guinea, little trouble was taken over the colour of Negro Cloth. Some may have been undyed or exported after little more than bleaching. And for those pieces that were dyed before export the palette was limited: 'White, Bleue, & Green plains for Negro Clothing' were the options specified by a Charleston merchant in the 1730s.[19] Many slave owners were hostile to any form of self-expression by their captives and had them dressed in deliberately drab costume. The South Carolina assembly took the trouble to set out permissible forms of dress in the 'Negro Act' it passed in 1735. Simple fabrics such as 'white Welsh plains' were commended; rich or gaudy materials, such as might be found in cast-offs from the master's wardrobe, were outlawed. It was a ruling that slaves constantly tried to subvert. An Angolan-born man in the colony embellished his 'white negro suit' with 'some blue between every seam, and particularly on the fore part of the jacket, a slip of blue in the shape of a serpent'.[20] In time, slaves turned the tables on their masters by exploiting uncoloured fabrics as a blank canvas to which vegetable dyes of their own devising could be applied. A visitor to one Georgia plantation in the 1820s reported that the inmates were kitted out in suits made of white Welsh plains in readiness for the winter. 'They prefer white cloth', he claimed, 'and afterwards die it of a purple colour to suit their own fancy.'[21]

'Shroesberry the Capital of Shropshire' may have been 'the great Markett' for Negro Cloth but the actual production zone was further to the west, in Wales. The changing organisation of the Welsh woollen industry in the eighteenth century is poorly understood, so too the means by which the product was marketed, but what is beyond doubt is that increasing numbers of rural dwellers in Montgomeryshire and Merionethshire came to be harnessed to the Atlantic economy. The labouring poor resorted to industrial by-employments in response to their 'growing dependence on the returns of day-labour and . . . the faltering cottage economy'. They were joined by small hill farmers who, faced by an 'economic terrain [that] became increasingly unyielding as the various demands of rents, taxes, rates and tithes outpaced returns from agriculture . . . looked to resolve their material difficulties through participation in the woollen industry'.[22] By mid-century parishes in the mountainous hinterland of Dolgellau and Machynlleth, the woollen-producing heartland, swarmed with spinners and weavers. Some hamlets registered surges in population growth that can only be accounted for by the employment opportunities offered by the woollen industry. Certainly, it is highly unlikely that the threefold increase in the inhabitants of Trefeglwys in the course of the eighteenth century is to be explained by major improvements in agriculture in that isolated Montgomeryshire parish.

Much of the export went by London, as it had done when Welsh woollens served European markets. When Henry Laurens, the South Carolina planter and merchant, visited the capital in the early 1770s he was confident that ample supplies of Negro Cloth would be available: 'Shall inspect Such parcels as are in the London Warehouses to Morrow or next Day', he told his partners in Charleston. If the current stocks were not satisfactory there was no cause for alarm, for fresh deliveries were never far off: 'parcels of Plains are hourly expected from Wales', he told one associate back in Charleston; 'a large Supply by Sea from Wales' was imminent, he told another.[23] Nevertheless, London probably played a less central role as the eighteenth century wore on. As the slave plantations became the chief destination for Welsh plains so Bristol became a more prominent port of despatch. Not only was Bristol a specialised Atlantic port, it was the place at which Welsh plains were transhipped from the river trows that plied the Severn to ships capable of navigating the open seas. Bristol could therefore furnish Negro Cloth directly and cheaply. As one Virginia planter warned his London correspondent in 1735, 'we want our Cloathing early for our slaves . . . wch will force us to correspond wth ye out ports; or let our slaves perish; or sit all ye winter by ye fire'. Besides, he added, 'all coarse woollens come Cheaper from thence'.[24] A contemporary concurred: 'Bristol is by much ye best place for such woolings they are 20 per Ct better'.[25] As the decades passed, factors from the out-ports usurped the position of dominance formerly enjoyed by the Drapers Company of Shrewsbury. Once, weavers had trudged with their cloth to local market towns; now, the agents of international cloth merchants came to them. 'The Liverpool Merchants have now persons on the spot, to purchase of the makers; and to assist the poorer manufacturers with money to carry on their trade.'[26] Cash advances were very welcome to the 'poorer manufacturers'; they were also a mechanism through which the factors could take control of the commodity. By enabling the makers to buy wool on credit, the factors had a stake in the cloth before it had been woven and a say in how it was finished. Ownership of the product had shifted from the weaver to the merchant capitalist. Abject proletarianisation came next.

Indeed, the fate of many of those who worked in the mid-Wales woollen industry was not enviable. Although Welsh plains were used to clothe some of the most savagely exploited human beings of the age, those who carded, spun and wove wool in the bleak uplands of Merioneth and Montgomeryshire were themselves subject to cumulative social and economic degradation. The rural population had turned to woollen production in a desperate effort to meet the increased rental demands of an avaricious landlord class. Much depended on the competitive strength of their product in far distant markets. As the eighteenth century drew to a close that strength became increasingly uncertain. The disruption brought about by the American Revolution was quickly overcome. In fact, trade in the 1780s was so buoyant that merchants in Barmouth established a special depot in which to house woollens for export. Renewed international war in the 1790s brought far tougher times, however. The conflict stretched on for a generation and was marked, in its later stages, by commercial embargoes that throttled international trade, especially with North America. Negro Cloth from Wales continued to circulate in Atlantic markets after the conclusion of the Napoleonic Wars, but with increasing difficulty. By the 1830s and 1840s the domestic woollen industry of mid-Wales was no longer spoken of as being either thriving or export-driven. The reasons for that have to be surmised. It may be that Welsh weavers were out flanked by rivals from industrialising New England, whose innovations in the making and marketing of cloth proved too competitive. The embargoes and counter-embargoes that had eventually brought the United States and Britain to war in 1812 not only choked off British exports, they acted as a great stimulus to American industry. Textile manufacturers in the United States were now well placed to take over domestic markets that had once been ceded to Welsh products. Writing in 1826, a Rhode Island manufacturer exulted in the fact:

The Sea Island Planters in Carolina & Georgia who used Welsh Plains
at from sixty to ninety cents that have tried our goods give [us] the
prefference and our orders for them this year are now nearly double
the last years & last year more than double the year before – we intend
making them as low as possible and selling them at small proffits to
regular customers.[27]

Conversely, some Southern planters remained loyal to the Welsh
product because of their reluctance to buy from Yankee industrialists as sectional divisions widened in antebellum America:
'You observe that my sales have been much lower than those
made elsewhere', a merchant in Charleston reported to his New
England supplier in 1832, 'which I very much regret, but the low
prices of Welsh plains and the political prejudices of our planters
operated much against domestics [i.e. Northern-made wool-
lens]'.[28] Such relief as this afforded was fleeting though, for
problems were massing on every front for Welsh woollens. It was
not only New Englanders who were forging ahead with high-
volume, mechanised production. They had been anticipated in
Yorkshire, the home of the Industrial Revolution in woollen
textiles. It is also likely that plantations, especially in the American
South, became more self-sufficient in the antebellum era. That,
at least, is the tentative suggestion made by two leading authorities in the area. That markets in the West Indies were depressed
by the 1840s is certain. The final emancipation of Britain's
Caribbean slaves in the 1830s introduced a degree of consumer
choice that had never been known under the old plantation
economy. Wherever they had the choice, ex-slaves gave up heavy
woollens for lighter and more comfortable cotton fabrics. The
mountain communities of Merionethshire and Montgomeryshire where domestic textile making was prevalent were plunged
into misery as a result. By the time of Queen Victoria's accession
the woollen-producing district that girdled mid-Wales recorded
some of the highest levels of pauperism in Britain.

In the summer of 1761 a young African boy arrived at Picton Castle in Pembrokeshire. The name given to him by his parents is not known; to his new Welsh master he was Caesar. He had been brought to Wales from Senegal, where he had been purchased by a British army officer called Captain Parr. The slave child, who had the appearance of being six or seven years old, was presented by Parr to Sir John Philipps, the owner of Picton Castle. What prompted Parr to make this gift is not clear, but Sir John would no doubt have been pleased with his acquisition. 'Black boy' servants were fashionable amongst the gentry of eighteenth-century Britain. They stare impassively from dozens of paintings, offering dishes of tea to their masters or holding the reins of a prized horse. Like Arab stallions, African house slaves were items of prestige consumption whose presence spoke of their master's wealth and worldliness. Their standard servant's livery was often embellished with exotic touches to give them an added oriental dash, like the velvet turban worn by young Caesar.

Sir John Philipps, whose prisoner Caesar became, was a politician of note. He was a major figure in the affairs of south-west Wales between his entry to the House of Commons as member for Carmarthen in 1741 and his death in 1764, when he sat as MP for Pembrokeshire. A regional magnate of his standing was precisely the sort of man whose household would have been adorned by a black attendant. (His equivalent in north-east Wales also boasted an African captive, for the baptism of 'Juba; a black belonging to [Sir] Watkin Williams Wynn of Wynnstay, Bart' was recorded at Ruabon parish church in December 1774.) Caesar, then, was not unusual in himself, but the timing and circumstances of his arrival in Wales are of interest because they stem from a particular moment of imperial expansion in the Atlantic world, and the distant events that led to Caesar's sojourn in Pembrokeshire were eventually to have significant consequences for the industrial history of Wales.

The Seven Years War (1756–63) was fought between rival European alliances. It was also fought out by two of the leading contenders, Britain and France, on a global scale. They vied for control of Indian commerce and the North American interior. They also, of course, tussled over the sugar islands, which were both rich and enticingly vulnerable. The seizure of trading stations on the African coast also had much to recommend it, hence the British expeditions against Saint-Louis at the mouth of the Senegal river and Gorée, an island just below Cape Verde, Africa's western-most extremity. The seizure of France's Senegalese forts in 1758 was a conspic-uous success for the British at a time when the war elsewhere was going very badly. Captain Parr, Caesar's captor, had served in this campaign. The slave boy was a souvenir.

The forts were to be permanently garrisoned rather than destroyed and the trading networks once exploited by the French would now work to the advantage of the British. The Senegambia region was a good source of gold, ivory and 'gum arabic' (a natural substance that was indispensable in the dyeing of linens and cottons). Permanent garrisons required supplying on a permanent basis, however; several hundred soldiers could not live off the land. The Treasury Board in London took the appropriate steps. In June 1758 it invited tenders from:

> any person or persons willing to supply the following sorts and quantities of provisions for four hundred men, viz. for each by the week, seven pounds of biscuits or soft bread, two pound and half of beef, one pound of pork, four pints of pease, three pints of oatmeal, six ounces of butter, eight ounces of cheese or four ounces of butter in lieu thereof; and likewise such quantities of rum, brandy or Vidonia wine as shall be judged necessary.[1]

The contract was awarded to Anthony Bacon, a London merchant. Bacon was a prosperous but not indecently wealthy trader. His winning of government contracts was to change that. The victualling contract for Senegal was the first of several, first in Africa, then the West Indies. Government work made Bacon immensely rich; it also made him a slaver. The ships he sent south with provisions, once emptied of their cargo, could be reloaded with local products, including enslaved human beings.

Atlantic trade was high risk. There were dangers everywhere – hurricanes and harvest failure on the sugar islands, over-stretched credit, volatile markets, privateers and pirates – but for those blessed with business ability and luck the rewards could be great. But what was done with those rewards? Some of the profits were ploughed back into overseas commerce, some creamed off for investment closer to home. Many entrepreneurs hedged against the hazards of trade by investing in government stock or real estate, converting the profits of colonial trade and plantation agriculture into fashionably rolling parkland in the Home Counties. Others took a different course; they invested in domestic industry. That is what Anthony Bacon did. Unlike those great merchants who indulged themselves with a Palladian mansion or a Gothick folly, Bacon did something that brought little in the way of social prestige. He built ironworks in south Wales.

Senegambia had been an exporter of slaves since the Portuguese first dropped anchor at the mouth of the Senegal River in the fifteenth century. In relative terms, the region had long ceased to be an important supplier to Atlantic markets; its semi-arid hinterland was too lightly populated to compete effectively with areas further along the coast. In the eighteenth century vastly greater numbers were shipped from the Bight of Benin or Angola. Even so, a steady stream of captives made their way to the coastal forts of Senegal to await an uncertain fate. Over 30,000 exited Africa in this way in the 1750s. It was no small trade. It made perfect economic sense, therefore, for Anthony Bacon to employ the spare carrying capacity he now had at Saint-Louis and Gorée in taking slaves to New World markets. Thus, the *Keppel*, which sailed from London in May 1759 with biscuit and beef for the garrisons in Senegal, was reloaded with a human cargo at Gorée. The fifty-two survivors disembarked at Charleston, South Carolina, in January 1760. Another of Bacon's ships, the *Sarah*, followed a few months later; eighty Senegalese slaves were delivered for sale along the Potomac River, the boundary between Virginia and Maryland, in November 1760.

As the Seven Years War came to a close Anthony Bacon extended his slaving operations. He became the co-owner of the 250-ton *King of Bonny*, whose name suggests specialisation in the commerce of the Bight of Biafra, more than 2,000 miles to the east of Senegal by sail. The ship's two voyages that are known to have been fitted out by Bacon did indeed go via Bonny. In the first, the *King of Bonny* left London in September 1764 and delivered 320 slaves to Barbados in April 1765. In the second, she sailed from London in March 1766 and disembarked 400 parched and emaciated Africans at St Kitts in October of the same year. Bacon was in need of slaves for he had secured additional government contracts, this time in the West Indies where, quite apart from the garrisons that stood in need of victualling, there were newly conquered islands to be made secure. Harbours had to be repaired and fortifications made good. For this, slave labour was required. Bacon agreed with the Treasury Board in

April 1764 to supply slaves to the island of Grenada. A further contract of January 1765 had him furnishing 'seasoned, able and working negroes' for government work on Grenada, the Grenadines, Tobago, St Vincent and Dominica. He was to be paid 27s. 6d a month for every male slave supplied, plus a daily food allowance of 31/2d per man. By 1770 Bacon's man on the spot, his junior partner Gilbert Francklyn, had put over 400 slaves to work for the government; they were 'very ill used' and died off even more quickly than their fellows in the cane fields.[1] At the handsome rate Bacon and his associates were remunerated that scarcely mattered. Between 1768 and 1776 Bacon and partners won government slave contracts worth nearly £67,000.

Anthony Bacon was clearly not squeamish about slaving. There was no reason why he should be. His whole life had been spent moving between different points in Britain's slave empire. He had been born in Whitehaven in 1717 or 1718. This spot on the Cumberland coast does not now seem a place of great commercial significance, but in Bacon's youth it was an important node of the Atlantic trading system. Coal seams ran beneath west Cumberland, a fact that was not lost on the Lowther family, the principal local landowners, who promoted a local coal industry with great vigour. The Lowthers also invested heavily in harbour facilities at Whitehaven so as to ease the export of coals to the burgeoning Dublin market. But coal was only the beginning. The Lowthers were intent on developing links between Whitehaven and the Chesapeake colonies as well. This was not because of heavy local demand for Tidewater tobacco, for there was none to speak of in their damp and isolated corner of the world, but because the Lowthers had ambitions for Whitehaven as a dedicated tobacco entrepôt. Tobacco could be landed, satisfying customs requirements that key colonial goods be sent exclusively to English or Welsh ports, and then instantly reshipped to foreign markets. Before the union of 1707 the major foreign market lay conveniently close at hand in Scotland. After 1707 the Lowthers simply re-orientated their slick import-export activities toward French and Dutch ports. In the 1730s and 1740s Whitehaven was second only to London in the importation of tobacco from the Chesapeake.

The tobacco trade gave Anthony Bacon his entry into Atlantic commerce. While still a teenager he left Whitehaven to take over a store on the Choptank River on Maryland's Eastern Shore, bartering European manufactured goods for tobacco. Bacon would have been aware of slavery even as a child, for the occasional slaving expedition left Whitehaven in the 1720s and 1730s, but on his arrival in the Chesapeake he was thrown into a fully fledged slave society. In the 1680s Maryland had followed Virginia in importing Africans in large numbers. Tobacco planters preferred them to English and Welsh servants; they were less costly and more easily brutalised. Maryland had just 1,611 slaves in 1680; by 1750 she had 43,450. Slaves, many of them born in Africa, were everywhere. Enslaved field hands clawed at the soil with hoes. Black lumbermen, sawyers and coopers prepared the immense hogsheads in which tobacco was packed for export. Slave boatmen plied the creeks and waterways of the Chesapeake, crewing the canoes, barges and skiffs that moved goods and people up and down the Eastern Shore. Even the store that Anthony Bacon took charge of would have had its own captive workforce. By 1740, when Bacon left the Choptank, still only twenty-two years of age, he would have been familiar with every aspect of a flourishing slave regime.

Atlantic slavery gave Anthony Bacon his commercial start in the 1730s. It remained the backdrop to his business dealings in the 1740s and 1750s: he continued to trade with the tobacco planters of the Chesapeake, including slave-owning notables such as George Washington. In the 1760s, when his fortunes took an enormous boost, it was because of slavery: the contracts to victual the slaving forts in Senegal, the contracts to furnish slaves to British islands in the Caribbean and the opportunity to participate first-hand in the slave trade itself. Anthony Bacon's entrepreneurial zest now seemed to know no bounds. In 1763 he became a partner alongside George Washington in the Dismal Swamp Company, an ambitious attempt to drain and cultivate the huge and ominously named morass that straddled the boundary between Virginia and North Carolina. Naturally, the immense programme of tree felling and drainage that this would involve was to be the lot of slaves, mostly furnished by Bacon. In 1763 Bacon also applied to the government for the right to lease coal mines on Cape Breton Island in maritime Canada, another British acquisition of the Seven Years War. Bacon had grown up amid collieries in Cumberland; he knew their value well. Indeed, he was already the owner of a mine near Workington.

Anthony Bacon now became interested in another coalfield, one a little closer to his London base than far distant Cape Breton, nearer even than Workington. The profits he had earned in the whirl of Atlantic warfare and commerce would be sunk in south Wales. In 1765 he began taking out leases on mineral property in the parish of Merthyr Tydfil in south Wales. This was the new frontier of the British iron industry. The coke-smelting technology that had been so famously developed by Abraham Darby at Coalbrookdale in 1709 had taken a very long time to move beyond its first small enclave in Shropshire, but in the 1750s it did so with explosive force. A burst of investment on the east Shropshire coalfield was replicated in Wales, where the mineral endowment was just as propitious for coke-fuelled methods. Blast furnaces began to spread along the northern outcrop of the south Wales coal measures where mineral leases could be obtained on bargain terms: at Hirwaun in the Cynon valley in 1757, then at Dowlais in Merthyr parish in 1759. Work on another blast furnace in the Taff valley – Plymouth, just south of Merthyr village – commenced in 1763. Bacon's furnace at Cyfarthfa was Merthyr's third.

Construction got underway in the summer of 1766. It was an immensely ambitious project. The furnace was to be state of the art. Anthony Bacon's partner was another Cumbrian, William Brownrigg, whose brother-in-law was to supervise the site. This brother-in-law, Charles Wood, was no jobbing builder, however. He was one of the most imaginative and innovative figures in the contemporary iron industry. He had devised a method of refining pig iron into malleable bars that used mineral coal rather than charcoal as was still standard in the trade. He had brought to fruition a mineral fuel package – smelting *and* refining – that would revolutionise the production of iron in just a few short years. Cyfarthfa in Merthyr was where this package was premiered. Coke smelting and coal-fuelled refining were brought together in a single, integrated unit. As the sponsor of this initiative, Bacon had propelled Merthyr to the very forefront of contemporary industrial technology.

Anthony Bacon's industrial empire in Wales grew rapidly in extent and sophistication. He bought up the Plymouth furnace in 1766, then Hirwaun in 1780. Bacon had need of extra smelting capacity, for in addition to the forge at Cyfarthfa he established a cannon foundry. The first evidence for this new activity comes from the minutes of the Board of Ordnance, the government body that commissioned guns for military service. Until the Seven Years War the casting of cannon had been restricted to the Weald of Kent and Sussex, the centre of Britain's heavy armaments trade since the sixteenth century. In the 1750s, however, the Board began to award contracts to gun founders elsewhere. The Board also began to look with favour on those who could cast guns from coke-smelted iron, which proved exceptionally well adapted for foundry work. Anthony Bacon, of course, had coke iron at his disposal. He had something else as well. He had access to a revolutionary new production technique: the boring of cannon 'from the solid'. The standard method of gun production was to cast them around a central core that could be removed once the metal had solidified. It was a method that brought with it the danger that air pockets could gather around the core, impairing the effectiveness and safety of the weapon. By casting the cannon as a solid piece of metal and then boring out the barrel Bacon was able to supply a more robust and more accurately finished product. The new-style guns were tested by the Board in 1774 and with favourable results: 'casting guns solid in the manner of Mr Bacon's is infinitely better than the ordinary way, because it makes the ordnance more compact and consequently more durable'.[2]

The new technique was not Bacon's, however. Boring 'from the solid' had been developed by John Wilkinson, master of the Bersham ironworks near Wrexham, and it was Wilkinson, having taken out a patent on the method, who actually manufactured the cannon that was delivered in Bacon's name. The association between Bacon and Wilkinson was one of mutual advantage. Wilkinson had technical expertise in plenty but he lacked metropolitan contacts and, being a notably abrasive character, had none of the diplomatic skills needed to acquire them. Anthony Bacon, on the hand, was by the mid-1770s an experienced government contractor who knew the ways of Whitehall. Yet the association between Bacon and Wilkinson was short-lived. So impressed were the officers of the Board with guns bored from the solid that they had John Wilkinson's patent annulled as contrary to the public interest. That gave Bacon the freedom to dispense with Wilkinson's services and set up a cannon foundry of his own.

Very quickly, Anthony Bacon became the foremost supplier of cannon for government service. The Board of Ordnance placed orders for 195 guns with him in April 1775, ranging in calibre from 6-pounders to 32-pounders. With hostilities breaking out in North America it was a good time to be a weapons contractor. As the war escalated so did orders from the Board of Ordnance. Bacon was commissioned to supply 561 artillery pieces in 1778. In 1779 warrants were issued for 396 more. The foundry and boring mill at Cyfarthfa must have been working flat out, as cannon were being supplied to the king of Sardinia and the East India Company, as well as the Board of Ordnance. Business was so brisk that Bacon took a new partner in 1777, the London iron merchant Richard Crawshay, who was to play a large role in Merthyr Tydfil's industrial future. In September 1782, however, Bacon informed the Board of his withdrawal from the gun trade. It was something forced upon him. Lord North's ministry fell in March 1782, brought down by the defeat of Britain's armies in America. It was replaced by an administration headed by Lord Rockingham, whose Whig faction had firm ideas as to what had caused the calamity in the colonies: the excessive influence of the Crown. This influence was exercised through tame MPs in the House of Commons who were happy to prostitute the national interest in return for pensions and other rewards – like armaments contracts. To counteract this malign influence the Rockingham Whigs trumpeted the need for 'economical reform'. Royal influence in the House of Commons was to be curbed by purging venal MPs. Government contractors necessarily fell into this category. Men who profited from contracts, the Rockinghamites maintained, should not hold positions of public trust. They had no love of their country, only a craving to 'suck her inmost vitals, to feast on her entrails, and finally glut their all devouring maws on her lifeless cadaver'.[3] Accordingly, Clerke's Act, passed in the summer of 1782, barred contractors from sitting in the Commons.

This presented Anthony Bacon with a problem. He was an MP, and had been for nearly twenty years, representing Aylesbury and New Shoreham, both of them conspicuously corrupt boroughs where Bacon's largesse had won him a following among the electors. Now he had the choice of relinquishing his political influence or his contracts. He decided to give up his contracts, but not before devising a way of circumventing Clerke's Act. Bacon complied with the new legislation by requesting the Board transfer his contracts to Francis Homfray, a Staffordshire iron-master. The transfer was more nominal than real, however. Homfray was to carry out the work at Cyfarthfa, renting the foundry and mill, and using only materials provided by Bacon. The contracts had passed to someone else but the proceeds still went to Anthony Bacon, MP for Aylesbury.

By the time of his death in 1786 Anthony Bacon had used the enormous wealth generated in the slave Atlantic to transform the prospects of the iron industry in south Wales. Profits made in the trafficking of humans were re-invested in new industrial applications in Wales, like coke smelting. Bacon was not the first to use coke in south Wales; that was the achievement of the founders of Hirwaun furnace (which Bacon later took over). Nor was he even the first in Merthyr Tydfil; Dowlais furnace predated Cyfarthfa. Nevertheless, Bacon, by deploying lavish amounts of capital accumulated in the slave Atlantic, was a catalyst for decisive change. The Dowlais Company had abundant reserves of coal and ore but not the funds to exploit them. 'We can find materials for six more Furnaces', one partner lamented in 1790, 'if we could find the Money to build them.'[4] It was not a problem for Bacon. The commerce in slaves had taken him into the ranks of the super-rich. With a surfeit of capital at his disposal Bacon was able to move into coke smelting on an extended scale, then into new areas that harnessed some of the most advanced industrial technologies of the time: Charles Wood's coal-fired refining method and John Wilkinson's cannon founding technique.

Anthony Bacon's contribution did not end there. He bought in his slipstream others who were to revolutionise the south Wales iron industry still further. After Bacon's death, the Cyfarthfa works were taken over by Richard Crawshay, his old partner in the gun trade, and taken to new heights. By 1800 they were the world's largest. Francis Homfray, the substitute cannon founder, returned to the English Midlands in 1784 but he had seen enough of south Wales to convince him of its potential. His sons Jeremiah and Samuel were installed as ironmasters at Penydarren, another new ironworks in the Merthyr parish in 1785. By 1802 the Homfray brothers gave employment to over 900 men, women and children at Merthyr – 'reckoning in the miners'.[5] Like Richard Crawshay, they went on to accumulate fabulous wealth.

Capital garnered in the slave Atlantic also transformed parts of north Wales in the late eighteenth century, courtesy of the Pennant family. The Pennants, in their later incarnation as barons Penrhyn, found their way to the House of Lords, but none of that subsequent eminence could have been anticipated when Gifford Pennant was born in the Flintshire parish of Holywell in the seventeenth century. Many decades later, Holywell would become a major centre of copper manufacture, as we know, turning out 'negroes' and 'neptunes' for the Guinea trade, but the 1640s and 1650s were lean years, offering few prospects to young men of the district. The paucity of local opportunity took Gifford Pennant to the Caribbean. Family tradition has it that he served in the Cromwellian conquest of Jamaica in 1655. There is no hard evidence for this, but Pennant was certainly present on the island in the 1660s, intent, as were many others, military veterans and hopeful migrants alike, on acquiring lands. He succeeded. By the time of his death in 1676 the Welshman had laid claim to 7,327 acres, mostly in Clarendon parish on the south of the island.

Gifford Pennant's lands passed to his son Edward, who added a further 1,000 acres to the patrimony. This was a substantial estate, even by the inflated standards of Jamaica's planter class. It was valued at £40,667 in the local currency on Edward Pennant's death in 1736. Many of the assets, of course, were flesh and blood. Edward Pennant owned 534 'negroes'. They were appraised as though they were cattle. The most valuable were skilled artisans like coopers, essential for making the giant hogsheads into which sugar was packed; they were valued at £60 each. Male field hands fetched a little less, and women were not worth half. At the foot of the list came the 'picaninies' – a corruption of the Spanish *pequeño nino* (little child) – who were valued at £5 each. They had potential, but who knew if they would live long enough to become field hands?

Edward Pennant's son and heir, John (d.1782), did not linger in Jamaica. He and his wife sailed for Europe just months after Edward Pennant's death. Like many other planters of their generation, they chose the life of absentees. The oversight of the plantations was left to managers and local attorneys. They were to ensure that the slaves were lashed into activity; John Pennant was to tot up the profits in his sumptuous townhouse on Hanover Square in London's West End. These profits were considerable. Contemporaries were awestruck at the wealth of 'West Indians'. They were right to be so. There was a massive disparity between the average physical wealth of men and women in England and Wales and the free white population of the Caribbean. In 1774, the wealth of England and Wales was equivalent to £42 per head. In the British sugar islands things were very different. There, free whites could command £1,054 per head.[6]

Jamaican planters were stupendously rich. Their chattel slaves, predictably, were ragged and hungry. The exact condition of the Pennant slaves cannot be ascertained, but an exceptional run of plantation records from Mesopotamia in the parish of Westmoreland, forty miles or so to the west of the Pennant lands in Clarendon, permits a detailed insight into slave well-being in the late eighteenth century. The results are sobering. The working careers of over 500 of Mesopotamia's slaves can be reconstructed between 1762 and 1831. Two-thirds served as field hands for some portion of their lives. To work in the field gangs was the most arduous form of labour. Gang members were condemned to 'cane holing', digging out the pits in which new shoots were planted. It was intensely gruelling and performed at a merciless pace. Field hands were expected to work in a locked formation, moving across the cane field in unison. The gang driver stood ready with his lash lest anyone tarry. Eventually, the cycle of planting would give way to the harvest, but this brought no respite. The cane had to be cut and processed very rapidly. Any delay in getting the cane to the mill would result in the sticky sap losing its all-important sweetness. Field hands and mill workers alike would have to work around the clock with scarcely an interruption.

It was toil that only the young and vital could bear, and even they were quickly worn down by the ordeal. Male field workers at Mesopotamia lasted an average of 13.2 years before being relegated, stooped and broken, to less onerous tasks like tending livestock. Their life expectancy was just 42 years. By contrast, those members of the plantation workforce furthest from the cane fields, female domestics, survived a decade longer on average, and male gang drivers, the most privileged section of the slave community, had a mean age at death of 56.[7] There was nothing exceptionally vicious about the regime at Mesopotamia; its absentee owners thought of themselves as conscientious stewards. The Pennants took a similar view of themselves. They prided themselves on being humane, responsible planters; but that self-image rested upon self-deception. They were long-term absentees who depended upon managers and overseers to manage their business – managers and overseers who had fewer illusions about the cruel necessities of Caribbean slavery. Chronic overwork was standard, not exceptional. As on any plantation, the veterans of the Pennants' cane fields shuffled into premature old age with ruptured muscles and ulcerated limbs – if they lived that long. The data are less copious, but what survives suggests a regime comparable to that endured by the slaves at Mesopotamia. An inventory taken at one Pennant estate, King's Valley, in 1807 lists 87 adult males. Of these, 65 (or 75 per

cent) were under the age of forty. Only two men on the plantation had managed to hang on into their sixties.[8]

The unremitting, industrial rhythm of sugar production was
sustained through terror. Nothing but the threat of gross physical
violence could inure workers to its demands. Any refusal to work
or any tardiness in complying with an overseer's commands led to
punishments of sickening cruelty. Abundant evidence is available
in the uniquely detailed diary of one overseer, Thomas
Thistlewood, who had charge of the Egypt plantation, close by
Mesopotamia in Jamaica's Westmoreland parish, between 1751
and 1767. Thistlewood never hesitated to reach for his whip. His
floggings often concluded with salt, lime juice or pepper being
rubbed into the victim's wounds – 'pickling', as the diarist called it.
The lash was only one of many torments. Other punishments
were more prolonged. Runaways from Egypt were regularly
confined to stocks ('bilboes'), to which Thistlewood added his
own refinements. One slave was fastened into 'the bilboes both
feet', whereupon Thistlewood 'gagged him; rubbed him with
molasses & exposed him naked to the flies all day & the mosqui-
toes all night'.[9] On other occasions slaves were forced to
participate in the degradation of others who had displeased their
master. When Hector mislaid a hoe in July 1756, Thistlewood had
another field hand urinate in his eyes and mouth. Hector himself
had only days earlier been made party to a still more loathsome
form of punishment, one inflicted on a recaptured runaway.
Thistlewood gave his prisoner 'a moderate whipping, pickled him
well, made Hector shit in his mouth, immediately put in a gag
whilst his mouth was full & made him wear it 4 or 5 hours'.[10]

To modern readers, Thomas Thistlewood's diary is a catalogue
of appalling sadism. Yet Thistlewood did not think of himself
as behaving in an unusually capricious or severe fashion. He
reprimanded the unmeasured ('frenzied') use of the whip by
inexperienced overseers. Nevertheless, he was clear in his own
mind that violence, often of the most ferocious sort, was essential to the plantation system. He was also aware that keeping
slaves in a state of absolute dread was the main guarantee of his
own security. Rebellions of the enslaved were endemic in eighteenth-century Jamaica, and Thomas Thistlewood would have

been mindful of the fate of whites whose vigilance slackened. He had no wish to follow 'Mr Graham', the overseer of 'Land Rumney' plantation (the estate founded by Henry Morgan of Llanrumney in the 1670s), whose decapitated body was found after an uprising in his district in 1765.[11]

Thistlewood's private actions, gruesome though they were, simply matched the routine savagery of public authority on the island. Rebels or persistent runaways were tortured as a matter of policy. Courts could order the cutting off of ears, the slitting open of noses and the branding of faces. Disfigurement was at the foot of an escalating tariff of judicial punishment, one that culminated in the roasting to death of rebel leaders over slow fires. Visitors to Jamaica admired the island's lush scenery, but it was in truth a landscape of blood, garlanded with the gibbeted bodies and severed heads of the executed.

Such was the source of the Pennants' wealth – wealth that was used by Richard (c.1737–1808), the latest Pennant heir, to renew his family's links with Wales. By his marriage to Anne Susannah Warburton, solemnised in the fashionable surroundings of Bath Abbey in 1765, he acquired a half-share in the Penrhyn estate in Snowdonia. Richard Pennant must have brooded on the economic potential of his Caernarvonshire lands, for as soon as he inherited his father's Jamaican plantations in 1782 he opened negotiations for the purchase of the other half of Penrhyn. He also paid a lump sum to the tenants of Caebraichycafn in exchange for their right to take slates from the small, seasonally worked quarries that dotted the mountainside. Pennant had a vision of something far more ambitious. The patchwork of little excavations was to be obliterated by a monumental new quarry. The mountains of north Wales must have appeared unprepossessing to an improving eighteenth-century landlord: bleak, drizzle-bound and with soils that were either too thin or too waterlogged. But those same mountains, if shattered into a million flakes of slate, could realise a fortune. Richard Pennant set about the task, using one fortune, that provided by his plantations, to unlock another.

Britain was in the midst of a building boom when Pennant became master of the consolidated Penrhyn estate. The decade that followed the end of the American war was one of headlong urban growth. 'The Number of new Houses building in this Kingdom are more than the most enlarged Ideas can Imagine', an American loyalist (and slaveholder) exiled in Bristol told his cousin back in South Carolina: 'the Numbers are beyond description'. Bristol, he wrote, had been abuzz with construction since his arrival in the city:

> I speak much within bounds in saying more than five times the
> number [of houses] has been built than you have in all Charleston &
> this is nothing compared to London ... God knows where the people
> cums from to Inhabit them yet the people say they are taken up as
> fast as they can Build them.[12]

Houses, of course, had to be roofed, and slate was the perfect roofing material: impervious to water yet relatively light when split into thin panes. As new street followed street on the edges of Britain's expanding towns and cities the demand for slates intensified. Richard Pennant took full advantage. Hundreds of quarrymen were employed to eat into the mountainside at Caebraichycafn. As they did so, huge sums were expended creating a transport infrastructure that could convey the slates to market. In the 1790s an entirely new harbour was built at the mouth of the River Cegin and a new road laid down to connect Port Penrhyn to the quarry. By 1801 a horse-drawn railway ran parallel. Caebraichycafn disappeared. In its place was a chasm known as the Penrhyn quarry.

Richard Pennant's business career was a resounding success. The Penrhyn quarry revolutionised the local economy and laid down the technological and organisational norms that other quarry capitalists would follow as they swept into north Wales in the first decades of the nineteenth century. Pennant kick-started the process that made north-west Wales into the world centre of slate quarrying. What the Pennants began at Penrhyn was repeated at Dinorwic, Nantlle and elsewhere in Caernarvonshire and Merionethshire. Stepped galleries were sliced into the mountainsides, leaving huge cavities behind, as though vast inverted ziggurats had been levered from the rock. The slates, split and trimmed into shape, were shipped off by the million to roof the new industrial world of the nineteenth century.

Richard Pennant, like many others of his generation, was a self-consciously 'improving' landlord and entrepreneur. Improvement was one of the watchwords of the age. The proper application of human ingenuity, it was felt, could bring about steady advances in agriculture, in industry and in commerce. New plant varieties could be perfected; heavier and healthier livestock could be bred. Canals could open up once landlocked and inaccessible districts; better built and better drained roads could quicken the pace and lower the costs of commercial life. Improvement, directed by men of education and public spirit, knew no limits. It was a notion to which Richard Pennant subscribed – literally, for he was a paid-up member of the Society for the Encouragement of Arts, Manufactures and Commerce. His whole career was an exercise in improvement. Port Penrhyn's 'commodious harbour, capable of admitting vessels of 300 tons burden', testified to that; so did the railway that allowed 24 tons of slate to be brought down from the quarry with 'expedition and facility' by just two horses.[1] The spirit of improvement was extended to the West Indies. Would there be any advantage, he asked his manager in Jamaica in 1782, in using ploughs to break up the soil in his cane fields? 'I think much negroe Labour may be saved by it.' Given that 'Cotton manufactures' were 'increasing greatly' in Lancashire, might not cotton seed be obtained and a trial crop planted? And in view of the high price of slaves, should not prizes be awarded to the slave women who produced the most children or the healthiest?[2]

As befitted an improver, Richard Pennant was active in public life. He first entered the House of Commons in 1761 when he was returned for a borough in Hampshire, but for most of his political career he represented Liverpool, then Britain's premier slaving port. His wife's family had influence in the town that was put to good use. First elected in 1767, at the age of thirty, he remained one of Liverpool's MPs almost without interruption until 1790. By the late 1780s, as his fiftieth birthday approached, Richard Pennant must have thought himself in tune with the spirit of the age. He was an enlightened landlord, a firm Whig in politics, the proprietor of an innovative slate quarrying business in Wales and the representative of one of the empire's greatest ports. But in 1787, Pennant – or Baron Penrhyn of Louth as he now was – found the very basis of his fortune under attack. The foundation, in May of that year, of the Committee for Effecting an Abolition of the Slave Trade had an electrifying effect on British politics. Richard Pennant, who was used to being an ornament of empire, suddenly found himself a pariah: a slave owner and the voice of a city reviled for its role in the slave trade.

Explaining this extraordinary political upheaval is by no means simple. Complex shifts in religious sensibility were involved; so too were changes in the intellectual climate more widely, changes that made slavery, once regarded as an unexceptional necessity, into something deeply disreputable. New areas of social science, like economic theory, cast doubt on the value of slave labour; new theories of psychology identified empathy with the wronged and mistreated as an essential human quality; and new ideas about social organisation defined individual liberty as an inherent human right. Some of these notions were articulated in 1792 by petitioners from Monmouthshire who denounced the slave trade as 'repugnant to the spirit and dictates of the Christian Religion, and a reproach to the Justice and Humanity of a liberal and enlightened Nation'.[3] When this petition was drawn up such ideas had intruded into the conventional wisdom of the age, but Christians had not always found slave trading repugnant, nor had the people of Monmouthshire always felt themselves to be part of an 'enlightened Nation'.

In the 1730s a small group of Welsh Baptists left the Delaware valley in search of a new home. Their forefathers had left Pembrokeshire and Carmarthenshire to settle in America a generation earlier, hoping to find there a refuge where they could practise their faith unmolested by the Anglican Church. The New World offered them religious toleration, but therein lay the problem; their own tolerance had its limits. This restless set of Welsh Baptists hankered after Calvinist exclusivity, but they found that doctrinal heresy was seeping into their church. They sought another new beginning, hoping to find it in the frontier wilds of South Carolina, far inland from the coastal plantation zone. This was the origin of their new community, founded on a meander of the Great Pee Dee River and soon known as the Welsh Neck.

The Baptist pioneers rolled south with the equipment they needed to overcome the harsh formative years: stores, farming implements and livestock. They also brought slaves. Admittedly, the Welsh Neck was not the rice-growing Lowcountry where slavery was fundamental. The Great Pee Dee slaves were few in number. David Harry brought three with him in 1738; Griffith Jones brought four.[1] They served mostly as farm hands, working directly under their flinty Welsh masters, who were themselves far removed from the languid planter class of Charleston. But if the Great Pee Dee slaves were exempt from the horrors of the Lowcountry they were slaves nonetheless, locked into a life of subjection and toil. And their Baptist masters saw no contradiction between their fiercely held Christian faith and the holding of men and women in bondage.

The willingness of Welsh Baptists to embrace slavery sits awkwardly with some commonly held notions about Atlantic slavery and its abolition. We are accustomed to think of slavery and Christianity as antithetical. After all, the most conspicuous campaigners against slavery in the last years of the eighteenth century were united by faith. William Wilberforce and his closest collaborators were evangelicals who were convinced that slave-holding was an egregious sin. Yet there was no necessary incompatibility between Christianity and slavery as an institution. The Old Testament is shot through with references to enslavement, few of them unreservedly hostile. The Israelites were advised that the enslavement of fellow Jews was permissible provided it was of fixed duration: 'If thou buy a Hebrew servant, six years shall he serve; and in the seventh he shall go out free for nothing' (Exodus 21:2). The use of others as slaves, on the other hand, was allowed without limit.

> Both thy bondmen, and thy bondmaids, which thou shalt have, *shall be* of the heathen that are around you ... And ye shall take them as an inheritance for your children after you, to inherit *them for* a possession; they shall be your bondmen for ever. (Leviticus 25: 44–6)

An acceptance of slavery continues in the New Testament. The apostle Paul instructed those members of the early church who were slaves to bear their fate with resignation, for all Christians, whatever their condition in this world, were in thrall to Christ. '*Exhort* servants [i.e. slaves] to be obedient unto their masters', he wrote in his epistle to Titus (Titus 2: 9).

Moreover, the Bible seemed to give explicit endorsement to *African* slavery. The book of Genesis tells how Ham, the son of Noah, was cursed for shaming his father. Or rather, punishment fell upon Canaan, the son of Ham, who was made subordinate, with all his descendants, to Noah's dutiful sons, Shem and Japheth. The patriarch pronounced a fateful sentence: 'Cursed be Canaan; a servant of servants shall he be unto his brethren' (Genesis 9: 25–7). The sons of Noah, of course, were charged with multiplying and being fruitful after the flood that they alone had survived; they were the point of origin for all subsequent humanity. Their different lineages dispersed across the world, so it was thought, and because the descendants of Ham were supposed to have populated Africa the Bible appeared to offer licence to those who would enslave them. Africans were the distant progeny of Canaan, and therefore condemned to serve those who God had blessed. The African slave trade, in this view, was nothing to be deplored. Its cruelties should certainly be curbed, but the reduction of Africans to servitude was justified by Scripture.

Virtually no one – not even Quakers, who were to supply the organisational backbone of later abolitionist agitations – spoke out against slavery because of their Christian faith in the first half of the eighteenth century. Nor were there many, in the Protestant world at least, who fretted over the salvation of enslaved Africans. And amongst those who did, a concern for the redemption of slaves implied no criticism of slaveholders. The Reverend Thomas Bacon (*c*.1700–68), for example, who sought to attract slaves to his church on Maryland's Eastern Shore, was not in the least disturbed by slavery as an institution. In fact, this Anglican priest, sponsored by the Society for the Propagation of the Gospel in Foreign Parts, took a positively benign view of the slave trade. Preaching before an enslaved congregation in the 1740s, Thomas Bacon portrayed the Middle Passage as an example of God's mercy: 'Hath He not brought you out of a Land of Darkness and Ignorance, where your Forefathers knew nothing of Him', he demanded of his listeners, 'to a Country where you may come to the Knowledge of the only true GOD, and learn a sure Way to Heaven?'[2] Having been rescued from paganism and introduced to the blessings of the Gospel, slaves should respect the injunction of St Paul: '*You are to be obedient and subject to your Masters in all Things.*' Whether or not a master acted with Christian charity was irrelevant, Bacon reminded his audience:

> you are to be subject and obedient, not only to such as are *good*, and *gentle*, and *mild* towards you, but also to such as may be *froward*, *peevish*, and *hard*. – For you are not at liberty to chuse your own Masters, but into whatever Hands GOD hath been pleased to put you, you must do your duty.[3]

There was nothing here for a slaveholder to object to. And lest his sermons arouse any concern in that quarter, Bacon added a calming preface to the published text. Masters, he wrote, should be reassured that 'the direct Tendency *of the Gospel-Doctrine is*, to make their NEGROES the better SERVANTS, in Proportion as they become better CHRISTIANS'.[4] It was a message that would not have given the least qualm to the preacher's brother, the slave merchant and Welsh industrialist Anthony Bacon.

Yet within a few years of Thomas Bacon's death in 1768 misgivings about slavery were being expressed. Some of the anxiety was religious at root, but not all critics were spurred on by Christian faith. On the contrary, it was the utility of slavery as much as its justice that was being called into question. Indeed, the first call for a comprehensive scheme of emancipation in the British empire was grounded in policy, not righteousness. As it happens, it was the work of a Welshman, Maurice Morgann, a native of Blaenbylan in Pembrokeshire. Morgann (1725–1802) was no evangelical; he was a colonial administrator who owed his career to the patronage of Sir John Philipps of Picton Castle, the owner of the Senegalese slave Caesar (see p. 55). As a member of Philipps's circle of Pembrokeshire Tories, Morgann won preferment at the Board of Trade, the government agency responsible for the regulation of colonial commerce. In the early 1760s he, like many others in public service, was preoccupied with the future direction of the British empire after the sweeping military successes of the Seven Years War. What form should the greatly expanded empire take? One of the policy memoranda Morgann drafted was later published as *Plan for the abolition of slavery in the West Indies* (1772). In this, he set out a scheme for a complete, if gradual, eradication of slavery in the British Atlantic.

Maurice Morgann clearly had no love for slavery. It was contrary to natural law and cruel. But equally important, it was impolitic. Societies based upon human bondage were necessarily volatile. Morgann did not share Thomas Bacon's belief in the mutual compatibility of slaves and slaveholders. Rebellion was always latent. Masters knew this all too well, which was why insurrections were often followed by short-lived embargoes on slave imports. A surfeit of Africans, resentful and unreconciled to their fate, threatened the stability of plantation societies. But if an instinct for self-preservation led planters to curb their appetite for African labour, it was never for long. Sooner or later, greed would get the better of fear, and the shipment of slaves would begin again. It had to, most commentators agreed, because unfree labour was an unavoidable part of colonial life.

But what if slaves, for all their superficial advantages, were essentially inefficient? This was the question upon which Maurice

Morgann brooded. Was slave labour superior to that of free men? A growing body of opinion thought not. Adam Smith was to make the inherent superiority of free labourers a running theme of his landmark *Inquiry into the nature and causes of the wealth of nations* (1776):

> The experience of all ages and nations, I believe, demonstrates that the work done by slaves, though it appears to cost only their maintenance, is in the end the dearest of any. A person who can acquire no property, can have no other interest but to eat as much, and to labour as little as possible. Whatever work he does beyond what is sufficient to purchase his own maintenance, can be squeezed out of him by violence only, and not by any interest of his own.[5]

Free workers, by way of contrast, would respond to the incentive of high wages. The higher the rewards, the 'more active, diligent, and expeditious' workers would be.[6] Working for wages, Smith thought, encouraged labourers to be industrious and careful; coerced labourers were necessarily slothful and careless in the execution of the tasks assigned to them. Why then was slave labour so common? Smith had two answers: one concerned the psychology of slave holding, the other was related to the peculiarities of New World agriculture. Enslavement, Smith wrote, appealed to a regrettable defect in human personality:

> The pride of man makes him love to domineer, and nothing mortifies him so much as to be obliged to condescend to persuade his inferiors. Wherever the law allows it, and the nature of the work can afford it, he will generally prefer the service of slaves to that of freemen.[7]

The New World was where this passion for tyranny could run free because slaves were deployed in growing super-profitable crops like sugar and tobacco. The bumper returns on these semi-luxuries, which were sold on home markets from which foreign competitors were barred, could alone 'afford the expence of slave cultivation'.[8] But such conditions were artificial; where markets were not protected for the benefit of planters, as was the case with wheat grown in the mid-Atlantic colonies, free labour would prevail.

Maurice Morgann drew upon this gathering suspicion of slave labour. In the *Plan for the abolition of slavery in the West Indies* Morgann envisaged a new form of empire in which the risks of slavery ('merited carnage' for the master class) could be gradually reduced and free labour assume its rightful place as the default system of social organisation.[9] He had in his sights the territory of West Florida, incorporated into British North America in 1763. This was to be a laboratory in which to demonstrate that African workers could cultivate tropical cash crops as free labourers rather than slaves. Paradoxically, Morgann's plan for emancipation was to start with the purchase of slave children in Guinea, but they were to be shipped not to America but to Britain, where they would be trained in agriculture and crafts. Once equipped with the essential skills, the young Africans would be settled at Pensacola on the Gulf coast of Florida. Here, the newly liberated people would flourish. Morgann foresaw a golden future: 'the settlers will increase, they will cultivate, they will trade, they will overflow; they will, being freemen, be more industrious, more skilful, and upon the whole, work cheaper than slaves'. Pensacola would be a beacon, inducing planters to manumit their slaves: 'slavery will thereupon necessarily cease'.[10] From being a subversive menace within the British empire, black people would be reborn as worthy subjects of the crown.

Maurice Morgann's plan was never realised, of course. Whatever feasibility his proposals might have had ended with the American Revolution. The North American colonies seceded from the empire with Franco-Spanish military assistance and West Florida passed to Spain as part of the peace settlement of 1783. Even so, the proposals made in the Welshman's *Plan for the abolition of slavery in the West Indies* did have a post-war outcome of sorts. Early in the war, political expediency had prompted the British to offer freedom to the slaves of Patriot masters. When Lord Dunmore, the beleaguered royal governor of Virginia, summoned all loyalists capable of bearing arms to rally to him in November 1775 he added this to his proclamation: 'And I do hereby further declare all indented Servants, Negroes or others (appertaining to Rebels) free that are able and willing to bear Arms, they joining His Majesty's Troops as soon as may be.'[11] It was a neat stroke: his lordship invited the slaves of Virginia's rebel planters to rise against them and don British uniform. Hundreds took him at his word, some of them from the plantations of Patriot luminaries like George Washington and Thomas Jefferson. They were embodied in Lord Dunmore's 'Ethiopian Regiment' and saw service right through the Revolutionary War. Many others – women, children and others not fit for combat – also sought refuge across British lines, especially in South Carolina. At the war's end thousands of ex-slaves were clustered into the last few zones still occupied by the British, desperate lest they be returned to their vengeful former owners.

That was precisely what the peace accords signed in Paris provided for. The American delegation had insisted upon it. Fortunately for the 'Ethiopian' veterans and the throng of followers sheltering in New York, the recently appointed British commander was not prepared to betray them. When Sir Guy Carleton, who had a habit of disregarding instructions he disagreed with, met with General Washington in May 1783 he refused to renege on promises made to 'Negroes who had been declared free previous to my arrival'. He did not see that he had the 'right to deprive them of that liberty I found them possessed of'.[12] At Carleton's side as he made this declaration was his secretary, Maurice Morgann.

Washington, who knew that 'several of my own are with the Enemy', was incensed. Yet there was little he could do: Carleton had already evacuated several thousand ex-slaves by sea. They were bound for Nova Scotia, the dumping ground for large numbers of destitute loyalists. Like other refugees, the discharged black cavalry troopers and sappers were to be granted plots of land in the chill surroundings of maritime Canada. The white loyalists who were also being settled in Nova Scotia did not look kindly on them. Some had been slave owners themselves and were keen to continue as such; a sense of racial superiority never left them. British officialdom was little better. The plots earmarked for black settlement were released slowly and tended to be in the least favourable locations. Not surprisingly, disenchantment with British freedom soon set in. By the late 1780s several hundred black loyalists were ready to entertain a far more radical departure – to Africa.

Maurice Morgann's scheme was known to Granville Sharp (1735–1813), one of a tiny band of anti-slavery activists at work in Britain in the 1760s and 1770s, who developed a strong interest in establishing a free-labour settlement for ex-slaves in the wake of the American War. Sharp was stirred to action by the plight of those ex-combatants who had made their way to London rather than Canada and who now had a visible presence, ragged and penniless, on the capital's streets: 'dark, coloured men', as a petition from six veterans put it, 'the unemployed, unprotected, & homeless Objects of Poverty, Want & Wretchedness'.[13] A committee for the Relief of the Black Poor took shape over the hard winter of 1785–6 to alleviate the suffering. Granville Sharp sympathised and joined with the committee's efforts, but he soon had in mind a far grander solution, one that extended beyond acts of local philanthropy, and one that would bring free-labour principles into play. He proposed a government-backed colony of ex-slaves in West Africa that would serve several purposes. It would remove a parcel of unsightly beggars from London and transform them into useful colonists. These colonists, by working the land with all the zeal of free labourers, would demonstrate to local potentates that cultivation by free tenants offered better returns than the export of human beings. As a consequence, the African coast would no longer be blighted by slavery. Instead, it would blossom as a source of cotton, coffee and sugar, all of them cheaper than their slave-harvested equivalents in the New World, and all thanks to British enterprise. A new empire in Africa, based upon free commerce and free labour, would rise to take the place of the shattered slave empire in the Americas.

Sierra Leone was selected as the first free-labour foothold on the slave continent, for where the first fleet of settlers sailed in April 1787. Their new 'Province of Freedom' was founded amid high hopes a month later. Inevitably, the more utopian expectations were disappointed. The settlers were inadequately equipped, the climate and soil were quite unsuitable for the cash crops they hoped to raise, and relations with local people were uneasy. Still less easy was co-existence with the British-run slaving station on Bance Island, a little way up the Sierra Leone river. None of that was known, however, to the black Nova Scotians who were now thoroughly disillusioned with the second-class treatment meted out to them in their place of exile. A group of them, under the leadership of Thomas Peters, who had served as a sergeant in His Majesty's Black Dragoons in the Carolinas, petitioned for their removal to Sierra Leone. Their wish was eventually granted. In January 1792 a fleet of sixteen vessels left Halifax, Nova Scotia, carrying 1,196 new emigrants to join the pioneers who had been transplanted from London five years earlier. Twenty years after the publication of *Plan for the abolition of slavery in the West Indies* circumstance allowed Maurice Morgann's scheme to be put into practice, but in reverse. Instead of Africans being brought to America to demonstrate the super-iority of free labour, as he had envisaged, Americans were transported to Sierra Leone to do so.

The new science of political economy, with its predilection for free labour, was not the only intellectual current in the second half of the eighteenth century that cast slavery in an ever more unappealing light. Enlightenment thinkers were apt to think of liberty as a 'natural right' and to hark back to the primitive freedom that, they supposed, humankind had enjoyed in the ancient forests. To live in society with others inevitably required the surrender of absolute freedom – mutual security demanded that violent and antisocial activities be outlawed – but the right to liberty was inalienable. Any surrender of freedom should only ever be partial and conditional. As Atlantic slavery was the most thorough violation of liberty conceivable, Enlightenment thinkers were inevitably hostile. The entry on 'The Slave Trade' in the *Encyclopédie* (1751–72) of Diderot and D'Alembert shook with indignation: purchasing 'Negroes to reduce them into slavery' was an affront to 'all religion, morals, natural law, and human rights'. Could it be 'legitimate to strip the human species of its most sacred rights, only to satisfy one's own greed, vanity, or particular passions? No ... European colonies should be

destroyed rather than create such misfortune!' The sentiment
was echoed in Britain, including Wales. As volume after volume
of the *Encyclopédie* appeared in Paris a somewhat less feted publication emerged from Carmarthen.

It is not too fanciful to see the *Pantheologia* (1762–79) of
William Williams as a distant cousin to the *Encyclopédie*, albeit one
driven by Methodism rather than the anti-clerical animus of
Diderot and D'Alembert. *Pantheologia* was ostensibly a history of
world religions, but its seven parts also describe the geography,
environment and history of the different continents at en-
cyclopaedic length. The author, William Williams (1717–91) of
Pantycelyn, Carmarthenshire, was a leading figure in Welsh
Methodism and a prolific poet, natural historian and writer of
hymns and devotional literature. He also stood forth as an opponent of the slave trade. The section of *Pantheologia* devoted to
Guinea condemned it as 'a traffick as can never be justified or
defended'.[14] Enslavement was in itself reprehensible, but New
World slavery was doubly deplorable because of the failure of
planters to spread the gospel among their bondsmen:

> agreeing among themselves not to make Christians of them, lest [the
> slaves] should understand that the Christian religion commands
> everyone to do as they would have others do unto them, and that as a
> result they should expect to be treated as humans, who have the same
> God and for whom the same Christ died.[15]

To demonstrate that Africans could be evangelised successfully,
William Williams also published a Welsh translation (1779) of
the earliest first-hand account of the Middle Passage to be
written by one of its survivors. *A narrative of the most remarkable
particulars in the life of James Albert Ukawsaw Gronniosaw, an African
prince, as related by himself,* first published in English in 1772,
described not only Gronniosaw's descent into slavery but his
subsequent conversion to the Christian faith.

William Williams of Pantycelyn was in many ways an arche-
typal Enlightenment figure: a prodigious author, an omnivorous
reader and a tireless activist. Most of that activism, of course,
was devoted to the Methodist cause; Williams Pantycelyn, as he
was known, spent many years as an itinerant preacher. He

reminds us that the Enlightenment and orthodox Christianity were not necessarily at loggerheads. Williams Pantycelyn could move smoothly between theological and scientific concerns without any sense that faith and reason were opposed. Rational observation could reveal the full majesty of God's creation – knowledge that would reinforce faith, not undermine it. The relationship between faith and reason was not free of friction, of course, and one end of the enlightened spectrum was occupied by heterodox Christians who doubted Christ's divinity, by deists who rejected the whole notion of Christian revelation and by outright sceptics who scoffed at all belief in supernatural power. Nevertheless, there was a substantial middle ground where Christian faith and enlightened understanding co-existed, and it was here that anti-slavery could flourish. Slavery was something that both troubled the Christian conscience and offended enlightened notions of individual liberty.

Religion *was* important in the campaign against slavery, but it is important to specify the ways in which it was. Context was everything. Famously, when an organised movement to outlaw the British slave trade emerged in 1787 its parliamentary spokesman was William Wilberforce, an Anglican evangelical. He provided the Committee for Effecting an Abolition of the Slave Trade with an irrefutably respectable public face. He signalled that the campaign enjoyed the endorsement of senior members of the Established Church, not just the support of socially eccentric sects like the Quakers. Anglican evangelicalism of the Wilberforce variety was not a major force in Wales, however. Methodism provided the revivalist thrust within Anglicanism, not Wilberforce's Clapham Sect. The Clapham zealots were wealthy and socially well connected; they had a preference for sober, undemonstrative piety. Above all, they had an instinctive reverence for the hierarchy of the Church. Welsh Methodism, by contrast, was socially mixed (and often humble), emotive and ready to work outside the established structures of the Church. The career of William Williams Pantycelyn testified to that. He was a tireless spiritual agitator who had a fractious relationship with the ecclesiastical authorities. If Wilberforce's brand of Anglicanism provided the newly formed abolitionist movement with high-level political influence at national level, it could not do so in Wales. As we shall see, the most noteworthy contributions to Welsh abolitionism came from outside the Established Church, from people sharply at odds with the Clapham Sect's profound social and political conservatism.

In the late 1780s abolitionism erupted into British politics. The Committee for Effecting an Abolition of the Slave Trade, well supplied with Quaker money, set to work with a will. Tracts were issued on a lavish scale. Over 15,000 copies of Thomas Clarkson's *Summary view of the slave trade* (1788), a digest of the most damning evidence, went out within a year of its publication. It was the opening shot in a propaganda barrage. No less impressive was the distribution of sermons, poems, prints, tokens, medals (like those bearing the famous 'Am I not a man and a brother?' design of Josiah Wedgwood) and other visual aids (like the nightmarish plan of the slave ship *Brookes*, jammed with African bodies). The public response was both instant and fervent. Friends of the slave trade were dumbfounded by the:

> number of people whose imaginations have been heated by harangues from the pulpit, and by advertisements in the newspapers … and by medals, with the impression of a naked human figure on his knees, bound in chains, and lifting his hands to Heaven.[16]

Committees sprang up in provincial towns and cities to press the case for abolition and to gather signatures for petitions to Parliament. The Manchester Committee led the way: a petition drawn up at the end of December 1787 had attracted over 10,000 signatures by the time it was sent off to London five weeks later. Copy-cat petitions cascaded into Westminster. Over 100 were presented to the House of Commons between February and May 1788.

Yet Wales was not well represented. Abolitionism made its strongest showing in the industrialising north of England and the Midlands, more often than not in rapidly growing settlements where the anti-slavery cause allowed emergent urban elites the chance of social and political self-assertion. These were places with mushrooming populations, well served by newspapers and printing houses, and thick with cultural and philanthropic societies that could act as scaffolding for the anti-slavery agitation. In Wales, where the population was relatively sparse, the urban tradition weak and print culture patchy, these favourable conditions were largely absent. Significantly, four of the petitions sent from Wales in 1788 came from a formal county meeting (those of Pembrokeshire, Cardiganshire, Monmouthshire and Montgomeryshire), the time-honoured conduit for petitions to the Crown or Parliament. These were gatherings of the county elites and respectable freeholders, not of the 'inhabitants at large' – even women – who flocked to add their signatures to petitions in English towns. The vibrant and innovative activism to be found there was less evident in Wales.

If the collective expression of anti-slave trade feeling was more difficult in Wales, where the cause was 'dogged by the political servility of the predominantly rural population', other initiatives were not.[17] The boycott of slave-grown sugar was one way in which individual households could show their support for Wilberforce's abolition bills. The West Indian lobby were scornful:

> Many ignorant People here have left off the Use of Sugar on the foolish Supposition that every Pound that is consumed costs the Negro that makes it an ounce of Blood. The Conjecture is ridiculous enough but many are Fools enough to believe it.[18]

Foolish or not, the boycott spread. It received early endorsement from a Baptist minister who was to prove the most strident and thorough-going Welsh opponent of slavery.

Achwynion Dynion Duon, mewn Caethiwed Truenus yn Ynysoedd y Suwgr ('The complaints of black men, in wretched slavery in the sugar islands') was a twelve-verse poem urging a consumer boycott of West Indian sugar, published in Carmarthen, perhaps as early as 1789. The author styled himself 'A Welshman opposed to all oppression'. Behind the pseudonym was Morgan John Rhys (1760–1804), a Baptist preacher who combined the most radical tendencies of the Enlightenment with millenarian Christianity. In Rhys's view, the American and French revolutions heralded the end of despotism. The new American Republic provided a model for the future (democracy and freedom of conscience), whilst the French Revolution had brought down Europe's most powerful absolutist monarchy. Reason was triumphant, superstition overthrown and universal liberty at hand. For a firebrand like Rhys, it was clear that the destruction of slavery was part and parcel of this consummation.

Morgan John Rhys enlarged on the topic in a sixteen-page pamphlet: *The sufferings of thousands of black men in Jamaica and other places, set forth for the consideration of the kind Welsh in order to try to persuade them to leave off sugar, treacle and rum*. He also saluted the colony for liberated slaves in Sierra Leone, which had just received an infusion of fresh settlers from Nova Scotia:

> It is to be hoped that this will be the means of opening the door for the gospel to be taken to the Negroes in their native land, and thus to put an end to their slavery and the cruel merchandize which has been so long a disgrace to humanity (viz. the slave trade), Amen, be it so.[19]

This endorsement came in the *Cylchgrawn Cymraeg*, the first political magazine in the Welsh language, which Morgan John Rhys began publishing in February 1793. Its agenda was libertarian, internationalist and combative. The *Cylchgrawn Cymraeg*, true to its editor's pseudonym, fumed against all forms of oppression. Conversely (and predictably) the American Republic was eulogised and the French Revolution hailed as a new birth of freedom in Europe.

February 1793 was not a propitious moment at which to rally to the cause of the French Revolution. Relations between Britain and France had deteriorated sharply after the overthrow of the constitutional monarchy in September 1792. The execution of the deposed Louis XVI by the new republican regime in January 1793 brought relations to breaking point. War followed ten days later. The harassment of Francophile reformers in Britain intensified accordingly. A hue and cry had already been raised against them in the autumn of 1792; with the onset of war they now bore the taint of treason. The crisis was a disaster for abolitionism. It was not necessary to be a radical to be an abolitionist – Wilberforce and his impeccably conservative Clapham Sect allies were sufficient proof of that – but radicals were, without exception, hostile to slavery. So, when radicals were stigmatised as subversives, abolitionists of all stripes suffered by association.

The shift in the political climate in 1792–3 was heaven sent as far as the slave trade's defenders were concerned. In the early months of 1792 abolitionism had still been very much in the ascendant. A fresh round of petitioning had been launched, aimed at overcoming the parliamentary obstructionism of the West India lobby. The public response was overwhelming, far greater than in 1788. The number of petitions grew nearly fivefold: 519 were presented to Parliament in just a couple of months, bearing the signatures of approximately 400,000 men and women. Wales was not excluded. The 'Gentlemen, Clergy, and other inhabitants' of Monmouthshire, for example, meeting at Usk on 10 March 1792, addressed the House of Commons in heartfelt tones:

> Impress'd with a lively concern for the unparalleled Miseries of our Fellow-Creatures, the Africans, and with an Abhorrence of the Cause of their Miseries – The Slave Trade – We take the Liberty to press upon the feelings and Justice of your Honorable House the Abolition of a Traffick that is repugnant to the spirit and dictates of the Christian Religion, and a reproach to the Justice and Humanity of a liberal and enlightened Nation.[20]

Nevertheless, when compared to England, Wales once again performed poorly, contributing just twenty petitions to the total – rather fewer proportionately than might have been expected. Welsh abolitionists could take comfort, however, from the fact that their cause was not only just, it was on the verge of victory. The 'West Indians' by contrast appeared beleaguered.

For several years supporters of the slave trade had been mounting a spirited but unavailing counter-campaign to that of the Committee for Effecting an Abolition of the Slave Trade. One energetic pro-slavery advocate was Gilbert Francklyn. Francklyn knew all about slavery; he had been Anthony Bacon's man-on-the-spot in the West Indies in the 1760s, superintending the 'seasoned, able and working negroes' that he and Bacon supplied for government work. Like Bacon, he was a member of the Committee of Merchants trading to Africa, the body that ran Britain's slaving stations on the African coast. Francklyn and Bacon went their separate ways in the mid-1770s: one began to shift his attention to Welsh ironworks, the other returned to the

Caribbean, where he harboured political ambitions. Bacon died in 1786, just before abolitionism reared its head, but Gilbert Francklyn was alive and ready to ride to the defence of slave merchants.

Francklyn's *Answer to the Rev. Mr. Clarkson's essay on the slavery and commerce of the human species* (1789) rehearsed what were to be standard arguments in defence of slavery. He berated the Abolition Committee's indefatigable agent Thomas Clarkson ('Rash and arrogant young man!') for claiming that Scripture was hostile to slavery. Did the puppy not know that enslavement was 'sanctified by the concurrent usage and approbation of the Patriarchs, Prophets, Apostles and Fathers?'[21] Indeed, was not the trade in Africans one that long pre-dated the arrival of the Portuguese on the Guinea coast in the mid-fifteenth century? And was not slavery a global phenomenon, known to most human societies, rather than the particular sin of West Indian sugar planters? Atlantic slavery, in other words, was historically nothing special. Besides, Francklyn asked, was there much of a *qualitative* distinction to be drawn between the enslavement of Africans and other forms of coercion that were generally agreed to be necessary? When the Royal Navy was in need of able seamen the press gangs went to work. Regrettable though it was, the pressing of free-born Englishmen was acknowledged to be essential for national security. The condition of British soldiers, Francklyn added, was no more enviable: they were flogged mercilessly for the smallest infractions. And did not common labourers in Britain, although legally free, endure lives of such hardship that their vaunted freedom was a mockery?

> Sure I am, that the labourer in England, who is the *slave* of *necessity* serves a harder task-master than the African finds in the West-Indies. No severities, there exercised, are equal to the cruelty of enticing poor people, by a small addition of wages, to work in lead, quick silver or other metals, or deleterious manufactories, which in a very few months, or years render the life of the poor victim an unremitting scene of torture and misery, which death alone can relieve him from.[22]

Did he have Anthony Bacon's Merthyr ironworks in mind?

Such arguments swayed only those who were already convinced of the value of slavery. Indeed, planters were bewildered at the failure of the general public in Britain to understand that hostility towards the slave trade – profitable and essential to the future well-being of the sugar islands – was threatening national prosperity, and doing so on nothing more than a sentimental whim. 'Those mistaken Zealots in the cause of liberty', a Welsh plantation owner was told by her agent on the island of Nevis, 'seem to discover a wish, by their ill-judged petitions, to deprive the nation of every resource ... their ignorance, and credulity, on this subject, [is] unpardonable'.[23] Richard Pennant, as MP for Liverpool and chairman of the influential Standing Committee of the West India Planters and Merchants, spelt out the economic consequences on the floor of the House of Commons in 1789:

> There were mortgages in the West India islands to the amount of seventy millions; the fact therefore was, if they passed the vote of abolition, they naturally struck at seventy millions of property, they ruined the colonies, and by destroying an essential nursery for seamen, gave up dominion of the sea at a single stroke.[24]

Despite all arguments to the contrary, the popular mood remained stubbornly abolitionist through 1790 and 1791. But the abolitionist tide, which had been running so strongly, was to ebb abruptly in the spring and summer of 1792, for it was at this point that the French Revolution, spiralling into its most radical phase, began to exert its decisive counter-influence. Pro-slavery propagandists, who had long argued that misguided attempts to reform slavery would bring chaos in their wake, seized their opportunity. The French Revolution, they argued, demonstrated all too clearly the dangers of tampering with established authority. Reform in France had brought bloody ruin in its wake; who could tell the havoc that would ensue if the same policy was applied to the far more volatile sugar islands? The West Indian interest had always argued that the merest whisper of abolition would loosen the ties that kept slaves in check: 'not the least of our fears is the mischief which an Apparent Triumph over their Masters may brew in the Minds of the Negroes themselves'.[25]

Events in the French colonies now seemed to bear this out. Saint-Domingue, the western portion of Hispaniola, the island that the French shared with the Spanish, was the richest sugar colony on earth. Almost half the world's cane was grown there, and a good part of the world's coffee. In 1789 Saint-Domingue was the envy of other colonial powers. Yet it was also fissured by complex antagonisms that divided the white elite (*grands blancs*), the poor whites (*petits blancs*) and the often wealthy but discriminated-against mulatto population (*gens de couleur*). The overthrow of the old regime in France allowed these tensions of class and caste to find open and increasingly violent expression as each of segment of the free population insisted that they (and they alone) were the local incarnation of the Revolution. Each segment found something in the revolutionary programme that appealed to them. The white elite clamoured for the abolition of the *exclusif*, the old regime regulation that compelled them to sell their sugar to metropolitan France; the *gens de couleur* demanded that the civil equality promised in the 1789 Declaration of the Rights of Man be extended to them; and the poor whites hoped that the Revolution would see an improvement in their miserably impoverished condition. The breakdown of political consensus in France, by spilling over into the Caribbean, had one further effect. It allowed one hitherto ignored constituency to find its voice: the submerged nine-tenths of Saint-Domingue's population, its 500,000 slaves.

The gigantic slave insurrection that exploded across Saint-Domingue's northern plain in August 1791 led many in Britain to conclude that the abolitionists were as soft-headed as they were soft-hearted. When the air crackled with fears of revolution, discipline not indulgence was the appropriate policy. 'Liberty Notions are spreading over all Europe', a Bristol merchant warned, '& I hear amongst the Negroes of North America. You have heard perhaps how dreadfully the French Part of Hispaniola has been laid waste by the Negroes.'[26] Black freedom was now associated with revolutionary turmoil rather than the earnest piety of Mr Wilberforce. When the godless Republic of Robespierre proclaimed the freedom of all slaves in the French colonies in 1794 (forty years ahead of British

emancipation) abolitionism was no longer just naive, it was unpa-
triotic. The ending of the British slave trade was off the political
agenda for the foreseeable future.

This was a time of despair for radicals like Morgan John Rhys.
With all hope of reform blighted he turned his thoughts to
emigration. Going to America had long been a cherished dream.
By 1794, with the leading lights of British radicalism in the Tower
of London or en route to Botany Bay, the young Republic offered
sanctuary. Like many other Welshmen of his persuasion, Morgan
John Rhys set sail for the west.

Landing at New York, he revelled in his bracingly democratic
new environment, so free from the fears and suspicions, the
arrests and proscriptions that disfigured his homeland. There
was a canker at work though, even in the home of liberty. Not all
Americans looked on the French Revolution with the same
approval as Morgan John Rhys; many, like President Washington
himself, looked askance at its bloody excesses. Rhys would have
none of it: it had been absolutely necessary that the 'ignoble
despots and vagabond priests' of the old regime be 'reduced to
men, [or] else banished and destroyed'. If the process had to be
accompanied by peals of 'divine thunder' and 'electrical shocks
which purified the air of such vermin', that is, the Terror, so be
it. The failure of many Americans to understand the logic of the
French Revolution was a consequence of a sinister compromise
within their own revolution: they had failed to extirpate slavery.
'Notwithstanding the Americans did much for the cause of
freedom', Rhys mused, 'they stumbled, as it regards the poor
African, at the threshold of equal rights.' France showed the true
way; if her path was followed 'universal emancipation must be
the result'.[27]

As Morgan John Rhys travelled the length of the eastern
seaboard in 1795 this conviction grew within him and he became
more strident in his denunciations of American slavery. The
wrath of God awaited those who would temporise with slave
holders. He demanded that Congress act: 'Legislators! Will you
wait until the cloud bursts on your heads? Proclaim the Jubilee –

you have no time to lose ... repentance will come too late.' The slaughter in Saint-Domingue stood as a warning – not of the dangers of reform, but of the reckoning that awaited anyone who tolerated slavery.

> Legislators of the United States! Are you ignorant of the signs of the times? You cannot be. The proximity of the West India Islands and the state of the Negroes, under the French Government, cannot escape your notice. But we have peace at home. Yes, Sirs! Where is the man barbarous and stupid enough to give the name of peace to the silence, the forced silence of slavery? It is indeed peace, but it is the peace of the tomb – the silence of slaves is terrible. It is the silence before the hurricane.[28]

Moving south into the slave heartland, Morgan John Rhys seesawed between exultation and despondency. He savoured the company of democrats, fellow Baptists and fellow Welshmen, whilst railing against human bondage and racially segregated churches. In January 1795, travelling through the Carolina back-country, he came to the Welsh Neck. He found there all the features that made him ambivalent about the United States. Preaching before a Welsh-American congregation, he found much to admire. His audience enjoyed lives of rural virtue along the banks of the Great Pee Dee, free from tithes and aristocracy. Yet there was the inevitable stain. 'They were attentive, but Achan (I mean Slavery) must be removed out of the Camp before there is any prosperity in the country.'[29] Morgan John Rhys had an indomitable optimism about America's future, but even he was coming to realise that rooting out Achan would be a monumental task.

By the middle of the 1790s abolitionists of all stripes, be they evangelical or radical, were at bay. Anti-Jacobin witch-hunting had driven most radicals out of public life; some, like Morgan John Rhys, went into exile. Evangelicals, with their deep social conservatism, were more comfortable with the deadened atmosphere of these years. Political life was not closed to them. Nevertheless, they were unable to reverse the marginalisation of abolition that the French Revolution and the insurrection in Saint-Domingue brought about.

Every fresh piece of news seemed to strengthen the hand of the West India lobby. On 4 April 1792 the government in Paris, lurching in a more radical direction, granted civic and political rights to all free males in France's colonies, regardless of colour. Saint-Domingue's *grands blancs* reacted with fury, turning abruptly against the Revolution: they had been against the *exclusif* but firmly in favour of their own exclusive privileges. The overthrow of the monarchy in August 1792 completed their alienation. The civil commissioners sent from Paris to impose the new order met, therefore, an uncertain welcome when they arrived in the colony in September 1792. The white elite now toyed with royalism or with independence. Thanks to the decree of 4 April the mulatto *gens de couleur* were sympathetic but they were militarily weak. The slave insurgents, on the other hand, whilst numerous and militarily potent, were fiercely opposed to the *gens de couleur*, whose acceptance of slavery was not far short of that shown by the *grands blancs*.

The position of the civil commissioners sent out by the National Assembly became still more precarious when Britain and France went to war in February 1793. An invasion from neighbouring Jamaica now threatened whilst the revolutionary regime was menaced by domestic enemies: white planters who were openly disloyal to the Republic and a host of armed ex-slaves. Drastic measures were called for; commissioner Léger-Félicité Sonthonax, who was a past member of the French abolitionist group *Les Amis des Noirs*, took them. He promised freedom to those 'Negro Warriors' who would come to the defence of the Republic. He was as good as his word. Indeed, on 29 August 1793 Sonthonax went further and decreed the freedom of *all* slaves in Republican Saint-Domingue. This momentous decree was subsequently ratified by Robespierre's government in Paris in February 1794. Toussaint Louverture, the most brilliant of the black generals, took note and rallied to the Republic.

Revolutionary emancipation was as abhorrent to Wilberforce and his fellow Evangelicals as it was to slave holders
themselves. It was also something that the British government
was determined to suppress before it could sweep over the
British sugar islands. William Pitt authorised armed interven-
tion in Saint-Domingue in 1793. By early 1794 the British had
occupied several strategic ports. They were welcomed by
white planters and not a few of the *gens de couleur*. Whether the
ultimate intention was to restore the old regime or to absorb
Saint-Domingue into Britain's own empire was not at first
clear, but either way it was plain that the re-imposition of
slavery on half a million human beings was now a British war
aim. War with Toussaint Louverture and his armies was the
inevitable consequence.

British abolitionism was thoroughly boxed in. The
campaign that had held out such promise at the start of the
decade fell to pieces. The Committee for Effecting an
Abolition of the Slave Trade gave up its permanent London
office in 1794. Actual committee meetings became fewer and
fewer. In 1797 they stopped altogether. William Wilberforce
continued to introduce parliamentary motions against the
slave trade but his attention turned to other matters.
Evangelicals had embraced the campaign against the slave
trade because dealing in slaves was sin, and so it remained, but
there were plenty of other sins to be addressed. The suppression of vice and the promotion of Christian paternalism in
Britain were not just worthy, they seemed far more feasible.

In 1799 Wilberforce introduced yet another motion to the
House of Commons calling for an end to the slave trade, his
twelfth in as many years. He did not bother to propose a thirteenth a year later. It seemed a fruitless gesture. A change in
the political context was required. When change did come in
the first years of the nineteenth century it came from an unexpected quarter: a captured Spanish island presided over by a
Welsh soldier, 'the blood-stained Governor of Trinidad'.[1]

A little after one o'clock on the afternoon of 18 June 1815 the Battle of Waterloo reached a critical juncture. After a lengthy cannonade the main French infantry assault began. From Napoleon's right the infantry corps of Marshal d'Erlon, 16,000 strong, began their implacable tramp up the low ridge along whose crest the allied lines were stretched. The first troops they encountered, a Belgian–Dutch light brigade, turned and fled with barely a shot fired. The next obstacle in their path, the division commanded by General Sir Thomas Picton, was rather more unyielding. Picton was a man upon whom Wellington could rely. He had earned battle honours aplenty in Spain alongside the duke and at Waterloo Picton was to add new lustre to his name. His peninsular veterans had already been through a day's hard fighting at Quatre Bras forty-eight hours earlier. He had helped save the day then, just as the cavalry of Marshal Ney seemed on the point of sweeping the field. It was not without personal cost: unknown to everybody but his aide-de-camp, two of Picton's ribs had been smashed by a musket ball. Broken ribs or not, the Welsh general – the Pictons were a Pembrokeshire family – was in the thick of things again on the day of Waterloo. As d'Erlon's columns thumped into the first of the brigades at his disposal and threatened to engulf it Picton put in himself in front of the second. Standing in his stirrups, he bellowed the order to advance. It was his last act before taking another French musket ball, this one fatal.

Sir Thomas Picton (1758–1815) was the most senior British officer to die at Waterloo. As such, his posthumous reputation was high. A monument was raised to his memory in Carmarthen in the 1820s and in 1859 his remains were removed from the family vault to be re-interred in St Paul's Cathedral, where his memorial stands close to Wellington's own tomb. He is the only Welshman buried in St Paul's. In Wales itself, he was claimed as a national standard bearer. The Edwardian city hall in Cardiff is home to a set of twelve marble statues: the 'Heroes of Wales'. Picton is one of them; he is an improbable companion to St David, a set of mostly forgotten medieval princes, Owain

Glyndŵr and Bishop William Morgan, who first translated the Bible into Welsh.

If, in afterlife, Picton acquired the aura of a Victorian hero his own life fell short of the chivalrous ideals the Victorians admired. His unflinching courage was beyond question – he had, after all, led the storm of the fortress-city of Badajoz in person – but in other respects he was lacking. 'I found him', Wellington said later, 'a rough, foul-mouthed devil as ever lived.[1] He was a roisterer, a duellist, a fornicator and, as his old commander noted, possessed of a famously abusive tongue. These defects were not unique to Picton, but there was also a singular stain on his character, one that stemmed from his years as military governor of Trinidad. Picton's regime (1797–1803) was brutally authoritarian, so much so that he was brought to trial in London for abusing his authority.

The Welsh soldier's appearance before the Court of King's Bench in February 1806, just as Parliament debated the future of the British slave trade, caused a political sensation. His actions in Trinidad, which did not stop at torture, focused public attention on the slave societies of the Caribbean. Was constitutional normality possible in such places? If it was, could it be built while slavery continued? Indeed, the tropical island that Picton ruled assumed an important place in broader arguments about slavery in the first years of the nineteenth century. The fate of Trinidad, it seemed to all sides, was to be the fate of the slave Caribbean in general.

Trinidad is the most southerly of the Lesser Antilles, lying just off the coast of present-day Venezuela. The island was claimed for Spain by Columbus in 1498 and it remained part of the Spanish empire for the next 300 years. The imprint of Spain was relatively light, however. It attracted few settlers and did not flourish. As an out-of-the-way and neglected colony Trinidad did not experience the sugar revolution that swept other Caribbean islands. The slave population remained correspondingly low. That was to change once the British seized the island in 1797. With the demise of Saint-Domingue as a major exporter of sugar, prices had reached extraordinary levels on the international market. The virgin interior of Trinidad therefore attracted covetous planters from across the Caribbean: French refugees who had escaped Saint-Domingue and migrants from long-settled islands like Barbados where soil exhaustion was pronounced. They flooded in; so did slaves as a consequence. In the last fifty years of Spanish rule just 4,625 slaves were imported, seeping in at an average of 93 per year. In the first ten years of British occupation 22,887 slaves were landed, an annual average of 2,289.

Picton greatly favoured the development of a slave-based plantation system and looked indulgently on the adventurers and eager investors who gravitated to the island. Indeed, he became a planter himself. He had known the petty privations of being a half-pay officer back in Pembrokeshire in the years after the American War; he cannot have been keen to repeat the experience. So, Picton bought up real estate and the slaves to work it. By the time of his departure from Trinidad, he was to claim, his investments were worth between £80,000 and £100,000. Even allowing for gross exaggeration on Picton's part, he had made a fortune. Much of it was repatriated to Wales to be used in the acquisition of an imposing mansion at Iscoed on the Tywi estuary. Such were the rewards of slave-based agriculture. The building of a plantation order had pre-conditions though. One was unremitting discipline. In this, Trinidad was deficient. A half-forgotten spot, it had long been a haven for runaways, deserters and desperadoes. Under Picton that was to change. He set about dispensing a brand of justice that was seldom tempered by mercy. The island's motley frontier population was cowed by a wave of exemplary executions. As for the growing numbers of forced African labourers, they were subjected to a slave code of Picton's own design. Delinquents who were not executed forthwith were despatched to the torture cells of Port of Spain's fearsome gaol to endure a range of grisly punishments.

The results of Thomas Picton's new regime were striking. Sugar exports totalled 8.4 million lbs in 1799; by 1802 they were 14.2 million lbs.[2] The price of slaves, always a good index of a plantation zone's buoyancy, shot upwards. Picton was in high feather. He had been equipped with powers that were little short of dictatorial ('You are supreme political, criminal, civil and military judge', an admiring Spanish planter told him) and he had put them to good use.[3] Stability had been brought to the island and the lassitude of former days had been replaced by vigour and economic growth.

Others had a different perspective, however. For abolitionists, Trinidad suggested the possibility of an alternative Caribbean, one without slavery. As an island where the plantation system had never been firmly established, might not Trinidad be used to demonstrate the effectiveness of free labour? And if the Spanish had not done so, could it be right that the British implant a full-blooded slave system? Wilberforce and his associates were determined to prevent it. Back in 1792 their opponents had defeated a motion for the abolition of the slave trade but at the cost of committing Britain to 'gradually' relinquishing the traffic in humans. The point at which the slave trade would be given up was repeatedly postponed, of course; it was, as far as the West Indian lobby was concerned, a pledge that need never be redeemed. A theoretical commitment to abolition, on the other hand, made it difficult to justify the active extension of slavery under the British flag. The abolitionists took full advantage of this. When, soon after news of the British seizure of Trinidad broke, William Pitt's government authorised the transfer of slaves from Britain's older Caribbean possessions to her new acquisition, Wilberforce strove to reverse the decision. He adopted a ploy that the abolitionists would use to great effect in years to come. Wilberforce downplayed humanitarian objections to the inter-island trade. Instead, he stressed how Britain's national interest would be impaired. There could be little sense in promoting the development of Trinidad if, as seemed likely, the island was to be returned to Spain at the end of the war. The argument struck home and the transfer of slaves from neighbouring islands, upon which Trinidad was at first reliant, was prohibited in 1799.

At the conclusion of peace in 1802, however, the British did retain Trinidad. This new circumstance required a change of tack by the abolitionists. James Stephen, who was Wilberforce's brother-in-law and his most tactically acute lieutenant, took up the challenge, supplying a new argument for restricting the slave trade. In *The Crisis of the Sugar Colonies* (1802) Stephen correctly foresaw that Napoleon's France would seek to reassert control over Saint-Domingue. The emancipation of French colonial slaves had been decreed in February 1794 when Jacobin revolutionary ardour had been at its highest pitch. The declaration of the National Convention in Paris, dated Pluviôse 16 of the Year II in the revolutionary calendar, was unequivocal: 'all men, without distinction of colour, domiciled in the colonies, are French citizens and enjoy the rights assured under the Constitution'. Eight years later the mood in French official circles was far more conservative. The high ideals of 1794 had come at a cost: the collapse of Saint-Domingue's export sector. It was not a price that first consul Bonaparte was prepared to pay any longer. His ambitions for a renewed French overseas empire required, so James Stephen reckoned, the restoration of slavery. That alone could bring Saint-Domingue back to its lavishly profitable former state. Sure enough, a vast armada left France in 1802 to bring the semi-independence of Toussaint Louverture and his black generals to a close. On its heels came a fresh government decree re-establishing the slave trade.

Stephen did not think it could be done. The experience of the British, who had attempted to conquer Saint-Domingue for themselves in the mid-1790s, had been telling. Not only had the former slaves mounted a ferocious resistance, but the invaders had been so ravaged by yellow fever and other tropical diseases that doubts were raised as to whether any European army could operate effectively in such a climate. For these reasons James Stephen denied that 'the infant Hercules of negro liberty could be effectually strangled in its cradle'.[4] Yet it would be a mistake, he warned his readers, to take comfort from France's impending defeat: the outcome would 'prove fatal in its consequences to our sugar Colonies'. Having liberated themselves, the one-time slaves would appreciate that

> the security of their own freedom would hardly be compatible with the continuance of negro slavery in all the surrounding Islands; and they would see in the bondage of Cuba and Jamaica, a yoke that

would be refitted to their own necks, if the powers of Europe should ever be able to replace it.[5]

The war of liberation in Saint-Domingue would necessarily sweep outwards and precipitate a revolutionary struggle right across the West Indies.

If the all-too-probable triumph of Toussaint's armies in Saint-Domingue threatened the downfall of Britain's own empire in the Caribbean, the outlook would scarcely be improved in the (albeit unlikely) event of victory for Napoleon's legions. The re-imposition of French authority could only be done on the back of massive force. Once secure in their possession of Saint-Domingue, the French would surely redirect their ample military resources to an attack on the vulnerable British islands. Either way, Britain's empire was imperilled. Stephen saw only one safe-guard: securing the allegiance of Britain's slave labourers by improving their treatment.

> The foundation then, Sir, on which alone I deem it practicable to build the future security of the sugar Colonies, is that of meliorating the condition of the great mass of the people, and converting them from dangerous enemies into defenders.

If the slave system was allowed to continue in its present state, Stephen insisted, it would 'be a source of internal weakness and danger till revolution or foreign conquest become the well merited result'.[6]

James Stephen now focused his argument on Trinidad. At a time when Thomas Picton was promoting the headlong expan-sion of plantation agriculture Stephen urged caution. The 'extension of our cart-whip empire' was, he declared, ill-advised in general. In the case of Trinidad, which was hemmed in by Spanish and French territories, it was especially foolhardy. 'To found a new slave Colony in that neighbourhood, seems to me scarcely less irrational, than it would be to build a town near the crater of Vesuvius.'[7] The 'colonization of Trinidada in the accus-tomed West India mode' should therefore be avoided at all costs. Stephen urged something quite different: the island should become a laboratory in which free trade and free labour were trialled. Trinidad could be recast as:

a most useful and important *entrepôt*, between the manufacturers of Great Britain and the traders of Spanish America. To Trinidada, the Spaniards already resort with their dollars and rich native commodities, in order to purchase the cottons of Manchester, and other manufactures of this country, so much in demand in their own.[8]

As things stood, this was a contraband trade, but if agreement could be reached with the Spanish an open, legal commerce would be even more profitable than slave-based agriculture. As for Trinidad's invitingly undeveloped interior, it should be settled, Stephen reiterated, by free labourers for reasons of security:

> *Let a portion of that rich and unopened soil, be sold at a low price, or granted freely, to all who will undertake, as the condition of the tenure ... to settle and cultivate it by the labor of FREE NEGROES.*[9]

In effect, James Stephen was reviving the argument that Maurice Morgann had made forty years before. The Welshman had hoped that West Florida might provide the setting for a free-labour experiment; the Englishman now put his faith in Trinidad.

James Stephen's vision of Trinidad's future could hardly have been further removed from Thomas Picton's. Unfortunately for the island's Welsh governor it was Stephen's view that was gaining ground in London. Picton had presided over an economic boom, it had to be conceded, but his methods were coming under increasing scrutiny in London. They were, it was concluded, unsafe.

In 1802 Picton was informed that the government of Trinidad was to be put on a new footing. Instead of exercising sole authority he was henceforth to be one of three commissioners: one military (Picton himself), one naval and one civil. The civil or first commissioner was to have seniority. Picton was not ready to share power with a civilian, least of all first commissioner William Fullarton, MP for Ayrshire and a man of relatively enlightened views. Fullarton's arrival in January 1803 marked Picton's effective demotion and led to an almost instant rupture between the two. It took no more than a month for Picton to resign in a fury. Fullarton's ways – punctilious, legalistic – were not his. Indeed, William Fullarton was scandalised by the state of affairs he found on Trinidad and wasted no time in setting up an investigation of Picton's regime, resulting in thirty-six charges being laid against the former governor. They included accusations of torture, false imprisonment and execution without trial.

When Thomas Picton reached London in October 1803 his notoriety had preceded him. Fullarton's charges were already under consideration by the Privy Council. They could be neither ignored nor dismissed. The ex-governor was arrested soon after his arrival in the capital and bailed for the enormous sum of £40,000, but it would be two years before his trial opened. The lengthy delay allowed a lively public controversy to develop, propelled forward by a succession of pamphlets, placards and squibs. The Picton camp hailed the former governor as an honourable British officer whose no-nonsense approach had been absolutely necessary; Fullarton's supporters assailed Picton as a tropical tyrant, who had ridden roughshod over the constitutional safeguards to which British subjects were entitled. Picton, it was sneered, 'bred among the goats on the mountains of *Wales*', was incapable of appreciating the 'immortal fabric' of the 'constitution of *England*'.[10]

When the matter came to trial in February 1806 attention was focused on one issue above all others: the torture of a young mulatto, Louisa Calderón, once the concubine of Pedro Ruiz, a merchant in Port of Spain. It was alleged that Calderón had colluded with another lover, Carlos González, to rob Ruiz. The facts of the robbery were not disputed; all that was lacking in the view of the Spanish magistrate was the confession of Calderón. This she stubbornly refused to make. Governor Picton was therefore asked to authorise the judicial torture of the accused. This was permissible under Spanish law, and Picton had been instructed to apply Spanish law when he had been left in charge of the island back in 1797. Accordingly, he signed the order allowing the investigating magistrate to 'apply the question'. The method of questioning was as follows. Louisa Calderón's left wrist was tethered to a pulley set in the roof of the torture cell;

her other wrist was strapped to her left ankle. When she was hoisted into the air by means of the pulley her remaining leg was left dangling. She was then lowered onto a sharpened spike set in the floor, her naked foot first, until her entire body weight rested on the spike. This was picketing.

Picketing – or 'Pictoning' as prosecuting counsel William Garrow suggested it should henceforth be called – was not the worst that Port of Spain's gaol had to offer, but it exercised a gruesome fascination for the British public. Prints purporting to illustrate Louisa Calderón's ordeal were in wide circulation. Garrow used one in court, showing the victim 'a drawing in water colours ... representing in striking manner her situation with the *executioner* and his attendants during the application of the torture'.[11] Garrow asked her to confirm its accuracy and after she had done so he flourished it before the jury. The frisson of horror that the episode aroused in court reflected the youth and sex of the victim. Calderón's age was never definitely settled, but she was certainly young: at the time of her picketing she was not long past puberty. The prosecution made much of her graceful femininity. Her entrance, in a demure white dress and a matching turban, was artfully choreographed. The contrast with Picton, who could never shake off his ruffian air, was unmistakeable. The general's protest that she was 'a common Mulatto prostitute, of the vilest class and most corrupt morals' could not dislodge the impression of injured innocence that the prosecution had contrived.[12] (Picton's outrage was more than a little synthetic: his own household in Trinidad had been presided over by a mulatto mistress who bore him four children.) Once the prosecution had satisfied the jury (quite incorrectly) that judicial torture was not sanctioned under Spanish law, the Welsh soldier's fate was sealed. The jurors returned a guilt verdict.

The trial of Thomas Picton shone a light upon some of the most unpalatable aspects of British colonial rule in the Caribbean. The torture inflicted upon Louisa Calderón could not match the atrocities visited upon Picton's slave victims, those who were burned alive or dismembered, but Calderón's sufferings were those of a young woman who was light-skinned and free. They were politically sensational. Unwisely, Picton's lawyers chose to contrast the supposed mildness of Calderón's treatment with the limitless agony to which slave prisoners were subject. They succeeded only in bringing the British public face to face with the shocking cruelty that was endemic across the Caribbean. By doing so, they extended the debate beyond the matter of Picton's individual villainy on the island of Trinidad; uncomfortable questions were posed about the validity of slave regimes in general.

Trinidad intruded further and further into the debate over the slave trade. A quiet step in the direction of eventual abolition was taken in May 1802 when George Canning MP acted upon one of the suggestions made in Stephen's *The Crisis of the Sugar Colonies*. Canning suggested that vacant lands on Trinidad, which the government proposed to auction off, be closed to slave-based agriculture. Free labour only should be permitted. This, Canning told the House of Commons, would comply with the vote of 1792 that had looked forward to the gradual abolition of the trade. To open Trinidad's uncultivated interior without restriction would mean a vast extension of the slave trade, not its tailing-off. Canning estimated the number of fresh Africans needed to bring Trinidad to the same level of development as Jamaica at one million. This was a subtle move. Canning played upon a latent division within the West India lobby. Slave merchants and the shipping interest were understandably keen to see the opening-up of a market that was, in the short term, boundless. British planters on the older sugar islands were less enthusiastic. The revolution in Saint-Domingue had sent exports from that colony plummeting from 93,000lbs of raw sugar in 1789 to just 18,000lbs in 1800. This had been greatly to the advantage of planters in Jamaica and elsewhere who had previously been outcompeted by their French rivals. Having seen sugar prices on the international market rear upwards because of Saint-Domingue's collapse, British planters were reluctant to see Trinidad's fertile and untouched acres bring prices tumbling back down.

When war with France resumed in 1803 a number of enemy territories fell quickly to British forces. One of these was a stretch of the South American coast a few hundred miles to the south of Trinidad. The under-used soils of Demerara (today part of Guyana) were as well adapted for sugar cultivation as those of Trinidad, and there was no shortage of investors hoping to rush slaves in. The abolitionists therefore reprised the arguments that had restricted slave sales in Picton's island. The enrichment of a few private individuals should never outweigh the broader national interest. A deluge of cheap sugar from Demerara would damage Britain's long-established colonies, and a rush of investment would bring no lasting benefits if the colony was returned to its former Dutch rulers at the end of the war. The argument hit home. After discreet lobbying from Wilberforce, Pitt prohibited slave imports to Demerara – and indeed, into any newly captured territory – by executive order in 1805.

The abolitionist leaders had now learnt that moral arguments against the slave trade were ineffective so long as the West Indians could pose as guardians of the national interest. A more serpentine approach, one in which the Guinea trade was shown to be contrary to British self-interest *and* morally indefensible, held more promise. James Stephen was already the master of this tactic. 'I earnestly request', he had written in *The Crisis of the Sugar Colonies*, 'it may be observed that my arguments have been addressed, not to the *conscience* of a British Statesman, but to his *prudence* alone'.[13] He returned to the theme in a new work, *War in Disguise, or, The Frauds of Neutral Flags* (1805).

On the face of it, *War in Disguise* had nothing to do with the slave trade. Writing in his professional capacity as an expert maritime lawyer, Stephen drew attention to a circumstance that prevented Britain making maximum use of her naval supremacy. The Royal Navy was able to clear the seas of ships from France and her allies but trade between Britain's enemies and their respective colonies continued without much impediment. The naval blockade was evaded quite simply by shipping colonial produce under a neutral flag, usually that of the United States. Sugar from the French islands was carried to, say, Baltimore, and then freighted – as American produce in an American bottom – to France. 'Buonaparte has recently boasted', Stephen wrote, 'that Martinique and Guadeloupe are flourishing, in spite of our

hostility.' Indeed, Stephen argued that tolerance of neutral shipping was actively damaging British trade. British-flagged
merchantmen had to run the gauntlet of enemy privateers,
adding greatly to losses and driving up insurance costs, when
neutral-flagged vessels could sail in perfect security. 'While our
colonies, and our colonial commerce, are labouring under great
and increasing burthens, those of the enemy, comparatively
unencumbered, are thriving at their expense.'[14]

There was not a breath of abolitionism in any of this; James
Stephen was arguing on patriotic grounds for the maximisation
of Britain's war effort. The conclusion he drew was that the
Royal Navy should impose a total blockade of enemy colonies,
intercepting belligerent *and* neutral shipping. A shift in policy of
that magnitude might have to be pondered at length by ministers,
for any general interdiction of neutral shipping would arouse
enormous American hostility, but the author of *War in Disguise*
suggested, almost in passing, the first practical step that might be
taken. It was that the importation of slaves into enemy territory
by neutral carriers be stopped. At first sight, this was not a
controversial proposal. Foreign shipping interests would be the
sufferers. But as Stephen well understood a prohibition would
have far-reaching repercussions for slavers sailing out of
Liverpool and the other home ports. A good many foreign-
flagged ships were in fact British owned, or British crewed, or
fitted out in British ports. Moreover, British-flagged ships themselves played an important, if little publicised, role in supplying
enemy colonies by landing Africans at neutral spots like the
Danish islands of St Thomas and Saint Croix, from where the
slaves could be transhipped to French, Spanish or Dutch territories. All of this was threatened by the Foreign Slave Trade bill,
which Stephen drafted early in 1806, just as the drama of Thomas
Picton and Louisa Calderón unfolded in the Court of King's
Bench.

The seemingly innocuous measure that James Stephen master-
minded was of very great consequence. Under its terms it
became an offence for British subjects to transport slaves to 'any
Island, Settlement, Colony, Plantation, Territory, or Place whatever' under foreign control. British subjects could not advance

capital or extend credit to foreign slave ships, nor insure them. Nor could such ships be fitted out in British ports. Abolitionists believed that the bill would disable at least half, perhaps three-quarters, of Britain's slaving fleet. The reaction of the slave traders suggests that their estimate was not too far wide of the mark. The protests of the slave ports made surprisingly little headway, however. The West Indian lobby's dogged obstruc-tionism had seen off Wilberforce's general abolition bills time after time, most recently in 1804 and 1805 when the veteran MP, encouraged by developments over Trinidad and Demerara, had resumed his annual motions for a cessation of the slave trade. The West Indians found it far more difficult to respond to the Foreign Slave Trade Bill. For one thing, pro-slavery MPs and peers found themselves in the awkward position of opposing legislation that was presented to Parliament as a measure for national security. Moreover, the Foreign Slave Trade Bill had been carefully framed by James Stephen, using what had by now become a favourite abolitionist ploy. He drove a wedge between the two constituent parts of the West Indian interest: the slave merchants on the one hand, the planters on the other. Stephen's bill was a grave threat to the merchants, but British planters were quite content to see their foreign rivals deprived of fresh slaves. Divided and weakened, the West Indians were powerless to prevent the bill becoming law in May 1806.

The end, when it came, came quickly for the slave traders. The hard core of West Indian support in Parliament had never been large, but pro-slavery advocates had been able to draw upon the broader sympathy of MPs and peers who were concerned about throwing away the economic advantages that the slave trade brought to Britain and who associated abolitionism with the programme of revolutionary emancipation adopted by France. By 1806 those advantages were lost to them. By restoring slavery in the French empire in 1802 Bonaparte had removed the grounds for supposing that abolitionism had any correlation with 'jacobinical' subversion. Abolitionism – or at the very least a desire to ameliorate slavery – could now take on patriotic overtones. Indeed, by embracing anti-slavery Britain's leaders could more easily differentiate their empire-building from that of Bonaparte. His was arbitrary and despotic; theirs was constitutional and liberal, founded on ideas of humanity and justice. Events had also put paid to another staple of anti-abolition propaganda, the suggestion that if Britain were to abandon the trade other countries would simply take up the slack. After Trafalgar the danger receded. The British now enjoyed overwhelming naval supremacy. 'Did we not ride everywhere unrivalled on the ocean? Could any power pretend to engross this trade', Lord Grenville demanded of his fellow peers when moving the Foreign Slave Trade bill, 'where we commanded from the shores of Africa to the western extremities of the Atlantic?'[15] Only the United States had the carrying capacity to take over where Britain left off but, as Grenville pointed out, there were moves afoot there to ban slave imports. (The United States was, as anticipated, closed to slave transports forever in 1808. What Grenville chose to ignore was the possibility of American carriers taking slaves to other destinations, which they did.)

Deprived of the fail-safe arguments of old, the West Indians were left exposed. Most slave trading had perforce already been abandoned, thanks to unexpectedly far-reaching effects of the Foreign Slave Trade Act. With the governing class now swinging behind abolition, popular enthusiasm for the cause was able to resurface. 'There had never been any question agitated since that of Parliamentary reform', one impassioned West Indian complained, 'in which so much industry had been exerted to raise a popular clamour, and to make the trade an object of universal detestation'.[16] When Grenville, the prime minister, introduced his bill for abolition early in 1807 no effective resistance was offered. The friends of the slave trade were routed, losing the critical vote in the House of Commons by 283 votes to 16. The Act for the Abolition of the Slave Trade received the royal assent on 25 March 1807.

James Stephen's calculated appeal to the prudence of Britain's rulers rather than their conscience had been vindicated. The slave trade, at least in its legal form, was gone. That is not to say that West Indian proprietors lost their existing slaves. They did not.

Slavery as an institution proved resilient; so too did Thomas Picton. His lawyers secured a retrial in June 1808 at which the legality of torture under Spanish law was established. This led the jury to return a verdict that recognised both the legality of torture as a Spanish practice *and* the illegality of Picton's behaviour as a British governor, adding for good measure that 'no malice existed in the mind of the defendant against Louisa Calderón independent of the illegality of the act'.[17] It was a convoluted and equivocal judgement but it was exoneration enough. Picton resumed his military career and did so with great success.

Spain was his redemption. By the war's end in 1814 Sir Thomas (as he now was) had received the thanks of the House of Commons on seven occasions. From 1813 he was a member of that House, having been elected for the Pembroke boroughs. When he was hurriedly recalled to arms in 1815 Picton was as socially settled as a man of his raw temper could be: the master of an estate in Carmarthenshire and a legislator for his country. His death at Waterloo put an end to his short-lived retirement but it ensured his apotheosis. Quite apart from burial in St Paul's, Picton was to receive the ultimate imperial accolade: colonial frontier towns in Canada, Australia and New Zealand were named in his honour. The war hero was revered, the 'bloodsoaked governor' of a Caribbean slave island forgotten.

The abolition of the British slave trade in 1807 was greeted at the time as a mortal blow against slavery. There were certainly grounds for optimism. Taken together with the closure of the United States to slave imports on 1 January 1808, British abolition seemed to have narrowed the scope of Atlantic slavery considerably. But by most measures slavery remained in rude health. The legal traffic by British carriers may have ended but that did nothing to alter the status of nearly three-quarters of a million unfree labourers on the British sugar islands. The abolitionists had hoped that the choking off of slave imports would lead to the slow death of slavery itself.

The planters, they imagined, finding themselves unable to replenish their stock of slaves, would either shift towards free labour as a more effective mode of employment or improve the condition of their slaves in such a way that slave populations would reproduce naturally. Slavery, the abolitionists assured themselves, would either collapse of its own accord in the British sugar islands or else it would be softened so thoroughly as to lose its most objectionable features. By the 1820s, however, it was clear that neither had come to pass. The monitoring of slave populations in the British West Indies revealed a slow but discernible contraction since 1807. There had been no significant 'amelioration' of the slaves' lot. The planters, on the other hand, clung to slavery as fervently as ever. Free labour alternatives were left stubbornly untried. If slavery was really to die further action in Britain was needed.

A new body, the Society for the Mitigation and Gradual Abolition of Slavery, was founded in 1823 in recognition of this. One of its first actions was to press Thomas Clarkson, now in his sixties, back into service. The tour around Britain that the veteran campaigner undertook in 1823–4 had spectacular results: 777 petitions in favour of slave emancipation arrived in Parliament. Not all localities were receptive to his message though. Wales, which Clarkson had never before toured, proved a sore disappointment. Where the northern counties were not indifferent they were hostile. Clarkson was struck by the political timorousness of the common people: they were '*half a Century behind* those of South Wales, - and *a Century behind* those of England'. The influence of some landlords was predictably antagonistic: 'Mr Pennant, the Heir of Lord Penrhyn, a man of £50,000 a year in the neighbourhood is quite against us in consequence of being a very large West India Proprietor.' Things were little better in west Wales. Clarkson found the inhabitants of Cardigan mired in 'subordination and ignorance'.[1]

Swansea was one of the very few places in Wales to respond wholeheartedly to the renewed agitation of the

1820s and 1830s. A local anti-slavery society had been founded in 1822, headed by a coalition of local clergymen and manufacturers, with Joseph Tregelles Price of the Neath Abbey Iron Company to the fore. Another sympathetic local industrialist was Lewis Weston Dillwyn of Swansea's Cambrian pottery, whose father William Dillwyn had been one of the founder members of the Society for Effecting an Abolition of the Slave Trade back in 1787. Lewis Weston Dillwyn became MP for Glamorgan in the first House of Commons to be elected under the terms of the Reform Act of 1832. It was a moment of critical importance for the cause of anti-slavery, for Dillwyn was not the only parliamentary debutant hostile to slavery. The reformed House was in general far more welcoming of abolitionist proposals than its cautious predecessor – not least because it had to come to terms with a major slave rebellion, the 'Baptist War', that had raged across western Jamaica in 1831–2. The way was open for the Abolition of Slavery Act of 1833, which was passed with the enthusiastic backing of Lewis Weston Dillwyn (as his diary in the National Library of Wales reveals). Freedom came to slaves in the British Caribbean on 1 August 1834, although most of them were consigned to the half-way house of 'apprenticeship' in which they remained tied to their existing plantations for a transitional period. That 'vile substitute for freedom' (to use the words of Swansea's 'Friends to the Emancipation of the Negroes in our Colonies') was only brought to an end in 1838 after much further protest.[2] By then the slave owners had already pocketed the generous compensation offered to them. George Hay Dawkins-Pennant, the heir to Penrhyn estate, walked away with £13,870, equivalent to £11.1 million today. His 764 Jamaican slaves entered freedom with nothing more than the clothes on their backs.[3]

Slavery remained intact then in the British colonies far into the nineteenth century, just as it did in the territories of other colonial powers. These others (the Spanish, the French, the Dutch and the Danish) showed a marked reluctance to follow the British path. It required the revolution of 1848 to bring about French emancipation. The Dutch waited until the 1860s, the Spanish until the 1880s. Nor were Anglo-American restrictions on the international trade taken up with enthusiasm by other nations. Slavers continued to sail in huge numbers under foreign flags, particularly those of Portugal and Brazil. Africans had first been shipped to Brazil in the mid-sixteenth century; in the mid-nineteenth century they were still being landed. Indeed, the flow of slaves into Brazil was accelerating not declining in the first decades of the nineteenth century. Over 241,000 slaves were landed in Brazilian ports between 1801 and 1810. Imports jumped to 327,000 in the decade that followed, then to an all-time peak of 431,000 in the 1820s. The flood of fresh Africans faltered slightly in the 1830s, but surged again in the 1840s when 378,000 entered the empire of Brazil. Only in the 1850s did the trade subside.

Indeed, slavery was on the march generally in the first half of the nineteenth century as new plantation frontiers were opened up. As before, slaves toiled to produce goods for people who enjoyed freedom: Europe's coffee-drinking, sugar-addicted consumers. But nineteenth-century slavery also had a new dimension: slaves worked to sustain European and North American industrialisation. The incessant rattle of textile mills in Lancashire depended upon the massive extension of cotton growing through the American South, and with it the extension of slavery. Welsh industrialisation was of a different character. For the most part it drew upon coal and iron ore wrenched from the ground locally. Welsh industry did impact upon one distant corner of the Atlantic world, however: Cuba.

The Gulf of Mexico emerged as a new storm centre of slavery in the first decades of the nineteenth century, sucking in bonded labour from far and wide. The mass movement of enslaved people within the United States was one aspect of this. Slaves were shifted from the old colonies around the Chesapeake and the Lowcountry to the new cotton-growing districts of the Deep South. The international slave trade into the US was gone, but the internal trade was booming. 'Every decade between 1810 and 1860', writes Peter Kolchin, 'saw more than 100,000 slave migrants.'[1] The westward march of slavery gave states like Alabama, which had not existed at the start of the century, a servile population of more than 435,000 on the eve of the Civil War.

As Anglo-American settlers moved along the Gulf coast they penetrated Mexican territory, where slavery had been outlawed in the 1820s. The prohibition was not to the liking of those who hoped to emulate the thriving slave economies of the Mississippi valley. Pro-slavery forces were intent on prising the lands north of the Rio Grande away from Mexico, and before long they succeeded in establishing Texas as an independent republic committed to slavery (1836) and in fomenting war between Mexico and the United States (1846–8). Yet the seizure of Texas was only the beginning for those who envisaged the United States as a slave empire spreading south and west. Southern militants hoped to repeat their success in Texas by staging further aggressions that would force the hand of Washington. The privately organised expeditions of *filibusteros* – crusaders for America's manifest destiny as a slave power – that were launched into Mexico and Nicaragua in the 1850s were one expression of this. There were also abortive invasions of Cuba in 1850 and 1851. Both were miserable fiascos, but the idea of annexing Cuba as a new slave state was one that greatly appealed to Southerners as the sectional divide deepened in antebellum America. 'The Pearl of the West Indies with her thirteen or fifteen representatives in Congress would be a powerful auxiliary to the South', one pamphleteer announced. It was not a view restricted to eccentrics. Senator Jefferson Davis, the future president of the Confederacy, was among those who insisted that 'Cuba must be ours'.[2]

Cuba bewitched Southerners because it had emerged as the new centre of Atlantic sugar production in the aftermath of the Napoleonic wars. The first two and half centuries of Spanish rule saw relatively little plantation development on the island. Cuba was prized more for its strategic than its economic value: Havana's magnificent natural harbour was Spain's principal New World naval base and the rendezvous point from which the treasure fleet, laden with American silver, sailed for Cadiz. Half the island's population lived in the city; much of the countryside was virtually empty. The contrast with the adjacent sugar colonies of Saint-Domingue and Jamaica, both teeming with field hands, was stark. Neither landowners nor officials could see any prospect of Cuban sugar forcing its way onto the international market. Cuban prospects were transformed, however, by the revolutionary struggles that convulsed the slave Atlantic at the close of the eighteenth century. Of these, the slave uprising in Saint-Domingue, the source of half the world's sugar on the eve of the French Revolution, was by far the most significant. The implosion of the French sugar sector in the 1790s opened up new opportunities for rival producers. Not all could take advantage, however. Most of the British islands were already worked to the limit; virgin lands, like those of Trinidad, were the exception rather than the rule. Cuba, on the other hand, had huge areas of unexploited soil. What was lacking was a workforce.

Cuba exported 32,000 tons of sugar in 1799. Fifty years later her sugar crop topped 290,000 tons, enough to supply a quarter of the world market. This dizzying rise was only possible because of a corresponding spike in the supply of slaves. Shipping Africans to the island, once a privilege restricted to politically favoured licensees, was thrown open to all comers in 1789. The results were striking. Over 240,000 slaves were landed at Havana between 1790 and 1821, when British diplomatic pressure brought the 'open' trade to a close. Official disapproval did nothing to halt imports though. The sugar boom required slave labour, so the inflow of *bozales* – as the newcomers were known

– continued unabated, but now through clandestine channels. In truth, slavers scarcely troubled to disguise their activities. The British consul in Havana estimated that 107,000 slaves were brought in as contraband in the years 1830–8.[3] The unfree population stormed upwards. It already stood at 286,900 in 1827; by 1841, just fourteen years later, the number of slaves had leapt to 436,500.

The new sugar plantations were concentrated in the west of the island, around Matzanas, where they were notable for the take-up of the latest technology: the use of steam power to drive mills was visible by the 1820s, railways had been laid down to take the sugar to port by the 1830s and vacuum boilers adopted to improve its quality in the 1840s. The onward rush of sugar cultivation was far less pronounced at the eastern end of the island. Even so, dramatic changes were underway in the Sierra Maestra above Santiago de Cuba.

The city that the English had sacked in 1662 remained, like much of Cuba, somnolent for the best part of the eighteenth century. The importation of slaves into the port can stand as an index of general economic activity. Years might pass without a single slaver entering Santiago's splendid anchorage. An English slave ship called in 1728; it was 1744 before another slave captain followed. Even in the later decades of the century, when Havana was booming as a slave port, Santiago remained quiet. Not a single slave was landed in Cuba's second city in the 1770s, the 1780s or the 1790s. After 1800, though, the pace of economic life quickened. The revolution in Saint-Domingue played a key role, just as it did in stimulating a sugar bonanza in the west of the island. Refugee planters fled across the narrow straits that separated eastern Cuba from the French colony, many bringing their slave workforces with them. In the cool uplands of the Sierra Maestra, high above Santiago, they found perfect conditions for the growing of coffee. A fresh wave of refugees arrived in the 1820s, this time from the mainland Spanish colonies (modern-day Colombia and Venezuela) where royal authority had been overturned in the wars of independence. The result, so the British consul at Santiago reported in 1833, had been a doubling of the city's population in the space of a generation and a 'consequent increase of cultivation throughout vast tracts of virgin soil admirably adapted to the culture of the coffee plant, the sugar cane, cotton, indigo and tobacco'.[4]

This spurt of growth was fuelled by slavery, it need hardly be added. Santiago de Cuba's slave imports, a statistical irrelevance in the eighteenth century, rocketed. Two slavers arrived in port in 1821; seven followed in 1822 and a further six in 1824. Nine slavers arrived at Santiago's quayside in 1825, almost all them from French ports, Nantes above all. (Technically, the French slave trade had been illegal since 1818, but slave merchants in Nantes paid little heed. Supplying the Cuban market became something of a speciality.) The boom slackened at the end of the 1820s, but slave importation continued at a lower, steadier rate through the next decade. John Hardy junior, the British consul in the city, estimated that 2,000 slaves had been landed in the province of Santiago in 1832 alone, and that since the profits realised ranged from 120 to 180 per cent there was little prospect of the trade perishing of its own accord.[5] Santiago de Cuba, in its own small way, was a new front in the advance of nineteenth-century slavery.

John Hardy junior did not dwell upon the fact – prudently, no doubt, as a representative of the nation that had set its face against the slave trade – but he was himself implicated in Cuban slavery. He had settled in Santiago de Cuba in 1829 as 'a Merchant and [the] principal proprietor of some valuable copper mines in its vicinity'.[6] The mines at El Cobre, high in the sierra, were indeed valuable. It was the mounting demand for copper ore in south Wales that made them so. Every ton extracted from El Cobre was shipped east across the Atlantic in specially constructed barques. These sturdy craft headed for Swansea Bay, where the ore was consumed in the giant copper works of the Tawe and Neath valleys. So urgent was Welsh demand that a workforce had to be assembled with great haste to excavate the ore. This being Cuba in the 1830s, opting for slaves was virtually a reflex action on the part of the mine's proprietors. But it was not the cruelty of Cuban slave masters that condemned hundreds of Africans to work in the shafts and galleries of El Cobre; it was Welsh industrialisation.

The copper smelters of the Swansea district had achieved global dominance on the basis of Cornish ores, supplemented in the later eighteenth century by those of Anglesey. By the early nine-teenth century, however, demand in Swansea was straining at the available supply. Parys Mountain had been worked out, Cornish output was not adequate to the demands put on it, despite climbing steeply in the 1810s and 1820s, and the importation of foreign ores was ruled out by heavy tariffs. In the late 1820s that changed: the tariff barrier was brought down, with immediate and spectacular results. Mining speculators scoured the world for ores to feed into the ever-hungry maw of Swansea's copper industry. Cuban ores were the first to be exploited.

Copper had first been excavated at El Cobre in the early days of Spanish rule. By the late seventeenth century, however, mining was so sluggish that the Crown, frustrated by ineffective private contractors, took direct control. The unfree workforce thereby became royal slaves (*esclavos del rey*). Cleverly exploiting their regal status, the slave workers quietly established themselves as an autonomous community, raising crops and herding livestock in mountain isolation. Such was the situation when John Hardy junior 'was induced, on visiting the neighbourhood for quite another purpose, to carry off some specimens of the refuse, thrown up from the old workings, in order to subject them to analysis'.[7] The sample ores proved to be of extraordinary rich-ness, 'some of them so rich as to afford not less than 53 per cent of pure metal'. The average yield was far lower:

> not more than 27 per cent; but even that proportion is so great as to ensure enormous profits to the proprietors, in competing with the produce of our native mines of Cornwall, where 10, and even 8, per cent are considered sufficient to afford a remunerating return.[8]

Ore like this could be shipped to Wales under the new tariff regime at a considerable profit. John Hardy and his London-based father of the same name, together with Cuban partners, re-opened the mine in 1830.

There were difficulties to be overcome, however. The Cuban partners were invaluable for the political connections they had – Joaquín de Arrieta of Havana negotiated a ten-year exemption from export duties for the company in 1832 – but they had little capital to offer. If the ore reserves of El Cobre were to be fully exploited, John Hardy junior and his local associates needed a massive infusion of overseas investment. This duly came when the original Cobre partnership assumed a much expanded, more heavily capitalised and majestic form: the Company of Proprietors of the Royal Copper Mines of Cobre, with its head office in London, at 26 Austin Friars in the heart of the City.[9] The reconstituted Cobre Company, as established in July 1835, represented a takeover by British capital. Or more accurately, the new company signalled the formal absorption of the Cobre mines into the Welsh copper industry. The London business addresses given by several of the new proprietors masked their Welsh industrial affinities. Mary Glascott and her sons, for example, who were listed as copper merchants of Great Garden Street in Whitechapel, might equally well have been described as the proprietors of the Cambrian copper works at Llanelli, for such they were. The solicitor Alexander Druce, who was to serve as the company's auditor, was a partner in the Llanelly Copperworks Company, the third largest concern of its type in Britain at that time. Charles Pascoe Grenfell (1790–1867), who was to serve as director of the company, had even stronger Welsh connections. Together with his half-brother and fellow Cobre shareholder, Riversdale William Grenfell (1807–71), he was a partner in Pascoe Grenfell & Sons, Swansea's most powerful copper combine of the nineteenth century.

The Grenfells were of Cornish descent, from the far west of the county where miners pursued veins of tin out beneath the foaming Atlantic. They were merchants and mine adventurers. Their association with Welsh industry began with Pascoe Grenfell (1761–1838) who became a trusted agent of the rascally copper magnate Thomas Williams. By his late twenties Grenfell was head of Williams's London office. In 1794 he tightened his links with his patron's family by entering into partnership with Owen Williams, the Anglesey ogre's son. Their plan, part-funded by Williams senior, was to buy up ores in Cornwall to supply the aging monopolist's smelting works at Middle Bank and Upper Bank in the lower Swansea valley. In time, the partnership took over the works, and when Owen Williams retired from business in 1825 the successor firm of Pascoe Grenfell & Sons was left as the dominant force on the east bank of the Tawe.

The other major mining concern at El Cobre, the Santiago Company, also boasted Welsh links. At its head stood William Thompson (1793–1854), the ironmaster of Penydarren, the Merthyr works founded in the 1780s by the Homfray family, the one-time associates of Anthony Bacon. Thompson's mighty fortune was based upon a combination of industrial investment in Wales and London finance. His uncle, another William Thompson, had invested in several ironworks in south Wales and the Wye valley in the years around 1800, of which Penydarren was the most important and enduring. The younger William Thompson inherited the holding in Penydarren (which he was soon to own outright) and an interest in his uncle's merchant house that marketed Welsh iron in the capital. This twin-track business – provincial industry plus metropolitan commerce – paid off handsomely. By the 1820s he cut a resplendent figure: he was a staggeringly rich ironmaster, a major figure in City politics (he was lord mayor in 1828–9 and MP for the City between 1826 and 1832), a director of the Bank of England and participant in a multitude of financial and shipping concerns. By investing in Cuba, Thompson was merely re-applying a well-tried formula: mineral exploitation and processing, in which he was well versed, would be allied to the London money markets. By the end of the 1830s the Santiago Company was in full operation, running a small fleet of copper barques out of Swansea: the *Alderman Thompson*, the *Sir Isaac Lyon Goldsmid* (named for the London financier who was Thompson's regular business associate) and the *Countess of Bective* (named for Thompson's only child, who had married into the aristocracy).

Just as the Cobre Company was closely allied with the Grenfell family at Middle Bank and Upper Bank, so the Santiago Company had its own Swansea associations, centred upon the powerful figure of Michael Williams (1784–1858). The Williams family, like the Grenfells, were of Cornish origin, and like the Grenfells they established themselves as industrial dynasts in the Swansea valley. Michael Williams, together with his father and brothers, was part of a consortium that took over the Rose Copper Works in 1823. Recast as Williams, Foster & Co, the partnership established a new smelting works in the early 1830s at Morfa, hard by the Grenfells' own Middle Bank and Upper Bank plants. The Morfa works was immense, employing 600 men, and it may be that the construction of this leviathan, plus the acquisition of new works in the Neath valley in the late 1830s, encouraged the Williamses to invest in Cuba as a means of securing adequate ore supplies. What is certain is that Michael Williams had charge of the Santiago Company's operations in Swansea.

Together, the enormously expanded Cobre Company (known as *La Compañía Consolidada* locally) and the Santiago Company poured money into eastern Cuba. What was now needed was a workforce to put it to work. The *cobreros*, the descendants of the slaves who been attached to the mines in an earlier era, could be ruled out. They had long campaigned for release from enslavement, and in the age of revolution their petitions finally met with success. Cuba simmered with revolt in the 1790s, and for the Spanish authorities, twitchily conscious of their proximity to the turmoil in Saint-Domingue, it made sense to temporise with the former *esclavos del rey*.

> At an imposing ceremony held on March 19th 1801 in Santiago de Cuba, in the presence of its Governor and the massed ranks of white and coloured militia, a royal decree was proclaimed recognising the liberty of the *cobreros*, guaranteeing them against re-enslavement and recognising their right to continue cultivating their lands.[10]

There would be no return to the mines for them. Muscle power and mining expertise would have to be found elsewhere.

Hard-rock miners who were schooled in the very latest mining technology were recruited from Cornwall, then a reservoir of skilled labour for the mines that were sprouting across Latin America in the 1820s and 1830s. The efforts of the Cobre Company to do so can be traced in the correspondence of Arthur Jenkins of Redruth, the company's agent who enticed scores of Cornishmen to emigrate in the 1830s. They were all to be experienced men – miners, carpenters, blacksmiths, ore dressers and enginemen – and all were to be of unimpeachable character. (Jenkins had a strong preference for fellow Wesleyan Methodists). They were sent out a dozen or so at a time. From Portreath on the north coast of Cornwall they sailed to Swansea, where they would board a copper barque headed for Santiago.

The Cornish provided a cadre of foreign experts; those who were to perform the most gruelling forms of labour were to come from elsewhere. Some were free immigrants from the Canary Islands or from the Asturias in peninsular Spain, but most were enslaved Africans. The British abolitionist David Turnbull, who visited *La Consolidada* in 1838 as a guest of John Hardy junior, was appalled at the discovery:

> We learned from Mr Hardy that the labourers employed were nearly nine hundred in number; but to our great regret we found that more than half of them were slaves, some the property of the Mining Company, and others hired out, as is not uncustomary, from their owners in the neighbourhood.[11]

In fact, considerably more than half the workforce was enslaved, as the census of 1841 revealed. At that time *La Consolidada* employed 750 workers, of whom 104 were foreigners (mostly Cornish), 167 were free people of Cuban or Spanish origin and 479 – or 64 per cent – were slaves. The Santiago Company employed 56 foreigners, 85 Cuban-Spaniards and 249 slaves – 64 per cent of the total.[12]

The treatment of slaves was in line with the usual Caribbean standards: brutal. The Cornish miners who were brought face to face with the savage realities of Cuban slavery were stunned by the experience. Cornishmen were no strangers to corporal punishment. Their native culture was one in which disobedient children were routinely beaten and certain categories of adult (criminals, sailors, soldiers) might be whipped severely. Even so, nothing prepared them for the violence they witnessed. 'The flogging of the Negroes in this country is most cruel', James Whitburn, a Cornish engineer confided in his diary, after witnessing the use of the feared cowhide whip that overseers carried coiled around their waists:

> I have seen them laid on the ground, sometimes tied to a ladder, and at other times held by one man at the foot and another at the head, while another Negro with a whip 10 or 12 ft long from the end of the stick to the point of the lash, gives the Negro confined 25 blows or I may say, cuts.

It was the sound that disturbed Whitburn: 'every blow rattles almost as loud as a gun. I have seen I think from 15 blows out of 25 to make cuts in the flesh from 8 to 12 inches long and open as if done with a knife.'[13] The flogging was not the end of it. The butchered victim was immediately fastened into stocks in 'a very painful posture ... their blood running from the cuts on the boards and ... [kept there] groaning as if in a fever'. James Whitburn also recorded the treatment of runaways. Great blocks of tropical hardwood 'from 40 pounds 50 pounds weight' were fastened to them by enormous chains of the sort that would be used for heavy haulage in England. 'The chain and block [together] I supposed to be about 100 lbs ... When they walk they take the chain in their hands, pluck it 2 or 3 feet at a time and walk on to perform their labour.' Whitburn was haunted by the hopelessness of it: 'Thanks God for freedom', he scribbled in his journal.

The English specialists were free from this sort of ill-usage, but freedom offered no protection against the tropical diseases that ran amok through the immigrant Cornish community: over one hundred – half the total – succumbed to yellow fever in 1837. James Whitburn's diary becomes a roll call of the dead. 'Ben Evans died', he wrote on 27 July, 'one of my particular friends, and eight others all in 12 days which caused me almost to despair of ever seeing my native country and friends again'. El Cobre had become a charnel house, and as news percolated back to Cornwall the lure of Cuba faded. Arthur Jenkins, the recruiting sergeant in Redruth, put as mild a gloss as he could on the crisis:

'The sickness and death which have occurred at Cobre since the commencement of the present year will I expect cause some shyness in the Minds of our Miners as to going there'.[14]

For all that the Cuban mines offered high wages, the dreadful attrition rate amongst Cornish miners choked back migration, causing the mining companies to seek out alternative sources of supply. Wales, where the mine proprietors had interests, offered an alternative, particularly in the early 1840s when economic depression narrowed opportunities at home. The *Merthyr Guardian* reported in March 1842 that:

> 30 miners and 2 blacksmiths left Merthyr on the 3rd instant, for the Island of Cuba, in the employ of Mr Alderman Thompson. With one or two exceptions they are single men, and their stipulation is for three years, or to be returned to Swansea should the climate not agree with them. They are to work in the Copper mines, the blacksmiths at £9 a month each, and the miners at £6, and to get one-half those wages during their voyages with provisions at the worthy alderman's expense.[15]

The Santiago Company, which William Thompson headed, also recruited in north-east Wales.

Welsh workers were generally cheaper than their counterparts from Cornwall. In 1835 Arthur Jenkins was hiring Cornish 'lumpmen' to sink the engine shaft at *La Consolidada* for £9 per month plus board and lodging, and thought the bargain a good one. Regular pitmen were even more expensive: 'as this situation is a step higher than that of a Lumpman ... I do not think that any competant person will be willing to go under £10 or 10 guineas per month with board &c'.[16] The Welsh lacked the hard-rock experience of men from Cornwall, as was frequently pointed out by the mine captains who took charge of them. Employees of the Santiago Company in 1843 were derided by the local agent of the Cobre Company as 'ignorant Welshmen who would be more properly described as labourers than miners'.[17] They were rewarded proportionately: £6 per month, or 30 to 40 per cent less than a Cornishman. Cheap they may have been, but the Welsh miners were no more resistant to yellow fever than their Cornish cousins. Thomas Price of Vaynor, who died at Santiago de Cuba in October 1842, may have been one of those shipped out from Merthyr by the Santiago partnership.[18] If so, he survived no more than five months in the Caribbean.

Not all Welsh migrants came off second best when compared to the Cornish mining experts; some were highly skilled smelters, hired to go to Cuba when *La Consolidada* began to carry out preliminary processing of the ore on the island rather than export it raw. The production of regulus, as the intermediate product was called, began at the end of the 1840s and necessitated the presence of accomplished technicians. As a rule, they were at the forefront of their profession; they were, accordingly, obituarised in the *Cambrian* of Swansea as they fell victim to tropical distempers. Charles Penrose, once of the Cwmavon copper works, perished in 1848;[19] Frederick Bankart, whose family owned the Red Jacket Copper Works at Briton Ferry, followed in 1862.[20] The regularity with which advertisements appeared for a 'steady practical Man, to superintend the SMELTING Department at the Cobre Company's Mines in St Jago de Cuba' tells its own story.

El Cobre had been transformed. In 1827, when the old mines were still inactive, there were fewer than 600 inhabitants. Of these, 514 were classed as *libres de color* – 'free people of colour', that is to say, the emancipated *cobreros* whose ancestors had worked copper ore in the seventeenth century. They lived alongside 35 *blancos* and 41 slaves. By 1841, with the mine re-opened, there were over 4,600 inhabitants and the number of slaves had grown forty-fold, most of them working for the Welsh copper companies.[21] Growth had come very rapidly in the late 1830s with the injection of British capital and mining expertise – and slave labour. It was a winning combination. Ore output at *La Consolidada* stood at 5,969 tons in 1837. Two years later, it was 13,874 tons. By 1841, output had roared upwards again; it now topped 25,000 tons.[22] The value of the company took the same upward trend. David Turnbull was told that shares in *La Consolidada* were being exchanged at £40 apiece on the London market when he visited El Cobre in 1838. The clear monthly profit was £12,000, equivalent to a 30 per cent annual return on the investment: 'a princely revenue', as Turnbull exclaimed.[23]

These monster profits continued for some years, despite competition from ore fields in Chile and South Australia. When the American writer Samuel Hazard came to El Cobre in the 1860s he found the working arrangements established in the 1830s still in place. 'Most of the captains are from England, and are practical miners, who have learned their business in the mines of Cornwall and Wales.' (Hazard evidently took Wales to be a region of England.) The 'assistants are generally also miners from the "old country"'. As for the labourers, they were still black people. The only novelty was the sight of Chinese indentured servants, whose presence was made necessary by the long overdue slackening of human imports from Africa in the 1850s.[24] Hazard left a vivid, if characteristically florid, description of the conditions a thousand feet below the surface in which slaves and *culíes* (coolies) toiled. The temperature was 140°F.

> Think of it, O ye who live in the light of day, in the midst of God's pure air, where, even on the hottest summer day, there is some gentle breeze to cool your burning cheek! – think of these human beings who spend their lives laboring in this heated obscurity.

Major change was at hand though, for Samuel Hazard's descent into the mine coincided with a sharp decline in its fortunes. The crash of the international copper market in 1866 permanently weakened Cuba's competitive position. By the time the market revived the initiative had passed to newer, low-cost producers in the United States and Newfoundland. By 1869 the Swansea-based *Cambrian* took it for granted that the great days of the Cuba copper trade were over. Cuban shipments had once been 'large and important', and had employed 'a large fleet of vessels [that] was regularly engaged in the copper ore trade'. Now things had changed: 'the importation of a cargo of copper ores from Cuba is regarded almost as a novelty, and almost everyone of the vessels which formerly traded to Cuba has been withdrawn and placed upon other stations'.[25]

Even so, for a generation the pull of Swansea's copper smelters had drawn Cuba into a close commercial relationship with Wales. It was a relationship with deadly consequences for thousands of people of African birth or descent. Just as the industrialisation of Lancashire held people in bondage in the cotton-growing states of Alabama and Mississippi, so the industrial supremacy of the Swansea region kept people captive in eastern Cuba. The strong abolitionist tradition in Swansea counted for nought. Indeed, the redevelopment of the dormant El Cobre mines was taking place just as that prominent Swansea citizen, Lewis Weston Dillwyn MP, was pressing for the abolition of slavery in the British Caribbean empire. The irony was unfortunate. But was it not unavoidable? After all, what jurisdiction did the British legislature have over Cuba? Parliament could not outlaw slavery in the territories of another sovereign power, as all but the most belligerent abolitionists had to concede. Besides, was not the British government taking every available step to curb Cuban slavery? A treaty was concluded with Spain in 1835, just as *La Consolidada* came into being, to crack down on the illegal traffic in Africans upon which the Cuban economy depended.

Yet the more that one looks at the link between Swansea and Cuba, the more the paradoxes multiply. In the case of the Grenfell family the contradictions become especially knotted and complex. It was the Grenfells who were the propulsive force behind much of the development at El Cobre. No one had a greater voice in the affairs of the mighty Company of Proprietors of the Royal Copper Mines of Cobre than Charles Pascoe Grenfell. So prominent a role did he and his half-brother Riversdale William Grenfell play that it is hard to see them as anything other than fully fledged Cuban slaveholders. Yet the Grenfell brothers, like their family at large, were evangelical Christians.

Pascoe Grenfell (1761–1838), the founder of the family's fortunes, was a close friend of William Wilberforce, and Wilberforce's influence induced him to speak out against the slave trade whilst an MP. (Pascoe Grenfell was first elected in 1802 and sat in the House of Commons for twenty-four years.) The next generation of Grenfells, the generation that invested in *La Consolidada*, were just as fervent in their evangelical faith. The family members based in Swansea were tireless in their good works. Riversdale William Grenfell built the Anglican church of All Saints in 1842 to cater for the community of copper workers at Kilvey. His brother Pascoe St Leger Grenfell (1798–1879) was still busier in promoting earnest Christianity in Swansea. He sponsored a barrage of evangelical initiatives in the 1840s and 1850s, when Grenfell influence in the area was at its height. He was a patron of the local Pastoral Aid Society (intended to fund additional Anglican curates in rapidly industrialising districts), the Swansea Religious Tract Society and the local branch of the British and Foreign Bible Society. Pascoe St Leger Grenfell, like most Christian philanthropists of his day, was also keenly aware of the need to take the Gospel to foreign parts, hence his support for the Church Missionary Society, and even the Society for Promoting Christianity amongst the Jews (something of a hobby-horse for mid-century evangelicals).

How did the Grenfells manage to combine this high-minded religious activism with a tolerance of Cuban slavery? Perhaps their ability to square the moral circle is a tribute to the impersonal blankness of joint stock companies, of which the Cobre Company (*La Consolidada*) was an example? Although family dynasties still loomed over the Welsh industrial landscape, for many Victorian entrepreneurs the family firm no longer appeared as an adequate vehicle for business. The family firm seemed particularly outmoded for ventures that required the marshalling of large amounts of capital, the creation of complex transport linkages and the coordination of operations across huge spaces – for ventures, in other words, like international mining. Joint-stock companies, which could mobilise capital on an immense scale, were ideally suited for this sort of enterprise. With their inscrutably neutral outward form, joint-stock enterprises were also perfectly adapted to veil many unpleasant realities. By severing the link between ownership and oversight that had been a feature of family capitalism the joint-stock form enabled brutal power to hide behind a decorous corporate nameplate. That is precisely what happened with the Cobre Company. For most of those concerned in the firm it was a collection of shares that passed to and fro on the Stock Exchange, scraps of paper that yielded a handsome dividend. The actual realities of El Cobre – the suffocating heat of the mine and the lacerated flesh of its imprisoned workforce – were obscured.

Such comforting self-deception may have been an option for the ordinary shareholder, but it was scarcely possible for those who were directors of the company and knew its inner workings. Besides, the involvement of the Cobre Company in slavery was soon to be made public. It was drawn to the attention of the British and Foreign Anti-Slavery Society by an anonymous British resident in Havana. A letter received at the Society's London headquarters in the summer of 1841 pointed out that Charles Clarke, the British consul at Santiago de Cuba, was also manager of *La Consolidada*, 'which is worked at this moment by 400 of the unfortunate victims of Slave dealing cupidity'. Clarke's predecessor as local head of the Cobre Company, John Hardy junior, had also been his predecessor as British consul. What did it do for British prestige, the Anti-Slavery Society's correspondent asked, 'when our own public officers contribute to the continuation of Slavery and the consequent degradation of our fellow Man?' Indeed, the recent appointment of known abolitionists to diplomatic posts in Havana would be set at nought if 'at the other end of the Island such men as Hardy and Clark [sic] were left at full liberty to wield the Cart-whip and the Cow-hide'.[26]

The British and Foreign Anti-Slavery Society lost no time in turning its fire on *La Consolidada* and other slave-holding British mining companies. When the Society petitioned Parliament in September 1841 against the continued involvement of British businesses in supplying or otherwise sustaining the slave trade explicit criticism was made of mining companies active in 'the Spanish island of Cuba':

> their mines are worked principally by slaves purchased by the agents
> of those companies; that the greater part, if not the whole of these
> victims of oppression have been illicitly imported into these coun-
> tries since the period when such importations were declared
> contraband, felonious, or piratical.[27]

There was a practical outcome. The petition of September 1841 gave rise to an act of Parliament, the Act for the more effectual Suppression of the Slave Trade of 1843. It was a law of startling ambition. It criminalised the holding of slaves by British subjects 'wheresoever residing or being, and whether within the Dominions of the *British* Crown or of any Foreign Country'. To plead that no local laws were being infringed – as the Cobre and Santiago companies might legitimately do in Cuba – was no defence. The Act imposed a universal standard, one from which British subjects could not depart. By doing so, the 1843 Act for the more effectual Suppression of the Slave Trade must rank as the foremost 'Welsh' contribution to global abolition. It is melancholy to reflect, however, that this contribution stemmed less from the ardour of Welsh abolitionism than from the success of Welsh industry in generating new and conspicuous hotspots of slave exploitation.

The Act for the more effectual Suppression of the Slave Trade, sad to say, did not end the use of slave labour at the Cobre mines. The Consolidated and the Santiago companies, barred from acquiring fresh slaves themselves, simply turned to hiring slaves from Cuban owners. There was no legal obstacle to leasing slaves, even if it was over such a long period of time as to be tantamount to purchase. Slave holders at El Cobre, as elsewhere, were incorrigible. Slavery in the mines declined only when the mines declined in the late 1860s.

The crisis of the Cobre mines coincided with the final years of the Atlantic slave trade. The last confirmed sailing for Africa took place in 1866 and delivered slaves to Cuba. There was not another. To the very end slavers adopted the latest technology in the pursuit of profit, using fast steam ships that could carry more than a thousand captives at a time, but the international context was now firmly against them. The defeat of the Confederacy in the American Civil War brought slavery on the North American continent to a dramatic close and introduced a new and decisive rigour to US naval interventions against suspected slavers.

Slavery was now on the back foot. The South lay in ruins, its slaves transformed into free men and women by the Thirteenth Amendment to the Constitution of 1865. In Cuba the outbreak of the Ten Years War, an anti-Spanish rebellion in the Sierra Maestra that began in 1868, weakened slavery from within. The rebels offered freedom to those slaves who would rally to *Cuba Libre*. The Madrid government was forced to respond in kind, and initiated a process of legal emancipation in 1870. Brazil, by then an (admittedly large) anomaly in a free labour hemisphere, followed suit in the 1880s.

This is to stray some way from Wales, but for good reason: Wales cannot be explained from within its own boundaries. This is true in all matters, but it is inescapably the case when dealing with Welsh involvement in Atlantic slavery. The canvas must be broad. It needs to stretch from the Gold Coast in the 1680s, where Welsh woollens were exchanged for slaves, to Cuba in the 1840s and 1850s, where captives laboured at the behest of Welsh industry. Wales, a tangible physical space in north-west Europe, gave rise to something more elastic, fluctuating and far-reaching: Slave Wales.

Slave Wales has a history that is uneven. That is not unusual; it is a quality shared with almost every region that was drawn into contact with Atlantic slavery. Different places played different roles in the Atlantic world, each with a different chronology. The seaborne trade in African slaves was over two centuries old before the English, and with them the Welsh, became involved. But when they did, Slave Wales was summoned into being: it supplied niche products to the slave Atlantic. Some parts of Wales stood aside, but others hummed with activity in response to the commands of the Royal African Company and the private traders.

Welsh exports were largely inanimate. Men and women did not migrate in large numbers to the slave world. The contrast with Scotland is strong. Scottish plantation managers and doctors were ubiquitous in the Caribbean. Irish migration also made its mark, with significant pockets of settlement in the Leeward Islands. Montserrat was Irish in the seventeenth century. There was no correspondingly Welsh island. Many individuals went, of course, like the three Williams brothers, bricklayers and stone masons, who left the Vale of Glamorgan for Jamaica in the 1770s and 1780s. They succeeded in easing themselves into the slave-holding class, rather to the embarrassment of their elder brother Edward Williams, better known by his bardic name Iolo Morganwg, who was an ostentatious abolitionist. Overwhelmingly though, it was commodities, not people, that left Slave Wales. Riches returned. The influx of Atlantic wealth found expression in industrial development of the sort pioneered by Thomas Coster, Anthony Bacon and Richard Pennant. It also took a more traditional form when planters and merchants invested in land for security or as a form of conspicuous consumption. Nathaniel Phillips was one who followed this route. He went out to Jamaica in 1759 as a merchant. He diversified into sugar planting and he prospered. By the time he left Jamaica at the end of the 1780s he owned three plantations and a live-stock pen in the east of the island, together with 706 slaves. That was enough to allow Phillips to retire to the Slebech estate near Haverfordwest: a mansion and 600 adjacent acres.

Such examples could be multiplied, no doubt, although to what extent is unclear. Slave Wales is poorly mapped. More often than not, its contours are indistinct. The production of Negro Cloth was clearly important, but exactly how important? Contemporary observers were struck by the spectacle of upland households in Montgomeryshire supplying the 'poor Negroes in the West Indies', but were they so struck that they overlooked equally substantial domestic markets? Likewise, there can be no question that Anthony Bacon made the single most telling *individual* contribution to the take-off of the Welsh iron industry, but was his type of investment – using funds accumulated in the slave Atlantic – typical? Slave Wales awaits its cartographer, someone who can record its landscape with thoroughness and accuracy.

The surveyor's task will be complicated by the fact that Slave Wales was not a fixed landscape; it shifted in shape and orientation. Negro Cloth was a major feature of the 1730s. By the 1830s that was no longer so, but by then Slave Wales had acquired a new and unexpected province in eastern Cuba. Such shifts were directed first and foremost by economic stimuli, but Slave Wales was contorted by political pressures as well. By the late eighteenth century Slave Wales provoked protest and resistance. Sugar boycotts and petitions sprouted from the soil. There were Welsh abolitionists who could be numbered amongst the most indefatigable of slavery's opponents; on the whole though, it is the relative indifference of the Welsh that stands out. The general conditions that inhibited abolitionism – the historic scrawniness of urban development, the poverty of print culture and the rest – are clear enough, but the failure of Wales demands further investigation. Once again, Celtic comparison throws up significant contrasts. The Scottish abolitionist tradition was significantly more robust, despite the eminence of Glasgow as an Atlantic port that was deeply implicated in the wider slave economy. Abolitionism was nourished by the Scottish Enlightenment and abetted by the Presbyterian Church, Scotland's established church, whose Evangelical wing was galvanised by the drive for slave emancipation in the 1830s. The fissiparous and poorly funded Dissenting congregations that cleaved to abolitionism in Wales exerted less leverage. Irish anti-slavery was akin to the Welsh: patchy and inconsistent. Irish abolitionists were fortunate in that the commanding political figure of the era, Daniel O'Connell, embraced their cause so wholeheartedly. Indeed, the 'Liberator' fought the general election of 1831 on the slogan 'Reform and Negro emancipation'. Yet anti-slavery was also a divisive issue. O'Connell's sincere commitment brought him into conflict with many émigré supporters. Emancipation did not sit well with the toxic racism to which Irish-Americans were prone.

The legacy of Slave Wales is complex and ambivalent. Atlantic slavery is long gone, but its residues dot the Welsh landscape. Slave Wales can be seen in the shattered rubble of abandoned slate quarries in the north-west. It is there in the ruins of Cyfarthfa ironworks, which rise up from the foundations laid down by Anthony Bacon. When walkers climb the spiral path that leads to the top of the now-landscaped slag tip at the old White Rock copper works a piece of Slave Wales lies at their feet. Other traces are more difficult to decipher. The poor weaving households of mid-Wales whose struggle for survival meant yoking themselves to Slave Wales are easier to detect from documents in Virginia and South Carolina, the destination for their Negro Cloth, than physical remnants in Montgomeryshire. Most remains of Slave Wales take this form: they are submerged or inscrutable. They require persistent interrogation. For every obvious landmark like Penrhyn Castle, the medieval fantasy built in the 1830s and 1840 on the rewards of slavery and slate, there are others that are reticent about their past. A mostly mute landscape must be made to speak.

To do so is necessary, for Slave Wales is no mere spectral presence, confined to a set of haunted landmarks. The legacy of Atlantic slavery is real and pervasive. An enormously expensive intercontinental business cannot flourish and endure for centuries without having a profound impact on world history. Just how profound is a matter of longstanding controversy. For some historians, taking their lead from the West Indian intellectual Eric Williams, slavery was fundamental in the coming of the modern world. The burden of Williams's path-breaking *Capitalism and Slavery*, first published in 1944, was that the profits of slavery and slave-based production were decisive for the Industrial Revolution in Britain. It was slavery that generated the extra investible capital required to achieve economic take-off. The opposing view is that slavery was eye-catching rather than essential. The slave trade and plantation agriculture made a very limited contribution to nineteenth-century industrialisation. It is quite easy, so adherents of this view allege, to think of Europe's industrial transformation proceeding on the basis of Europe's internal resources alone. (For more on this debate see the works listed in the section on 'The legacy of

Atlantic slavery' in the Guide to Further Reading that follows.)

The critics of Eric Williams and his school have unquestionably exposed weaknesses in the logic of his case and its chronology. In particular, his assertion that British abolition stemmed from a recognition that the sugar islands were in irreversible decline now appears untenable. The British sugar sector was highly profitable in the years leading up to 1807. Nevertheless, the emphasis that Williams gave to the *structural* centrality of slavery to the Atlantic economy has proved to be enduringly influential. Indeed, the rise of 'Atlantic History' in the last quarter of a century has renewed interest in the question. Current scholarship recognises that there was a critical Atlantic dimension to Britain's economic development in the eighteenth century.

- Slave-based tropical agriculture hastened commercial integration within the Atlantic arena by multiplying the number of ships at sea, by prompting improvements in dock and warehousing facilities on land and by the proliferation of associated service industries: chandlers, outfitters, stevedores, hauliers, shipping brokers and insurers.
- Atlantic commerce, in turn, drove forward new types of consumption. A high proportion of the slaves transported to the New World were set to work producing high-value substances like sugar, coffee and tobacco whose stimulant or narcotic effects were pleasingly addictive. This led to wealth creation for which there was no European precedent or parallel.
- This, in its turn, led to the diversification and deepening of domestic demand. For what was sugar without the spoons, nippers, bowls and tongs to serve it? Or coffee without a pot in which it could be brewed? Or tobacco without the jars or snuff boxes in which it was stored?
- Consumption on such a scale and in such variety was only possible on the basis of equally expansive production. New manufacturing and distribution networks rose together.

The Atlantic slave system encouraged the making of far more than the coarse woollens and scratchy linens with which the captive labourers were clothed; it underwrote the manufacture of articles intended for a genteel, comfortable lifestyle far removed from that of the labour camps in the Americas.

In these ways the slave Atlantic gave added buoyancy to the British economy – buoyancy that could have come from no other source. Wales was a beneficiary of this process and contributed its mite – a mite that was actually of strategic weight at different places and points in time. This is all too easy to forget because of the crushing impact that coal-based industrialisation had on Wales later in the nineteenth century. Coal came like a tornado, uprooting everything in its path and leaving an older landscape blasted and roofless in its wake.

But it is salutary to look back to before Welsh history took its carboniferous turn and to peer out across the western ocean instead. What happened in the slave Atlantic skewed all subsequent development in the world economy. Global inequity did not begin there, not by any means, but it began to assume a form recognisable to us. A single, crude comparison throws the issue into relief. In 1500 there was little to distinguish Western Europe and West Africa in terms of material culture and technology (except in specific, localised fields like, crucially for the slave trade, marine architecture). By 1850 the gap was immense and widening. The West became demarcated from the rest. North and South separated.

Much flows from this. Questions of policy and justice clamour for attention. Can Africa's chronic underdevelopment since the close of the slave era really be assigned to the legacy of transatlantic slavery? (If China and India can break out of margins to which Western imperialism consigned them, why not other regions?) Other questions follow. Did slave exports constitute an 'African Holocaust'? If so, should reparations be made to its victims? And how should African rulers who were complicit in the trade be judged? Subsidiary questions tumble out in turn. By whom, it is asked, should reparation be made? Hand-wringing and self-indulgent gesture will not assist here. Sober assessment and a consciousness of historical complexity will. It is a duty from which no one is exempt, north or south. Or, for that matter, east or west of Offa's Dyke.

Notes

Pages 1–3

[1] *Voyages: The Trans-Atlantic Slave Trade Database* (*http://www.slavevoyages.org*), voyage identification number 91093.

[2] *Voyages*, identification numbers 78128, 91519, 91520 and 91528.

Pages 5–12

[1] The words are from the title page of Charles Leslie's *A New History of Jamaica, from the Earliest Accounts, to the Taking of Porto Bello by Vice-Admiral Vernon* (London, 1740).

[2] Leslie, *A New History*, p. 119.

[3] NLW, Tredegar MSS and Documents 122, 'The State of the Stock The 31st December 1692'.

[4] E. A. Cruickshank, *The Life of Sir Henry Morgan, with an Account of the English Settlement of the Island of Jamaica (1665–1688)* (Toronto, 1935), p. 55.

Pages 14–28

[1] Thomas Phillips, 'A journal of a voyage from England to Africa, and so forward to Barbadoes, in the years 1693, and 1694', in *A Collection of Voyages and Travels, some now First Printed from Original Manuscripts, others now First Published in English* (6 vols, London, 1732), VI, p. 173.

[2] Ibid., p. 181.

[3] Ibid., p. 188.

[4] Ibid., p. 190.

[5] Ibid., p. 191.

[6] Ibid., p. 228.

[7] John Barbot, *A Description of the Coasts of North and South Guinea* (London, 1746), p. 44.

[8] K. G. Davies, *The Royal African Company* (London, 1957), p. 171.

[9] Phillips, 'A journal', p. 195.

[10] Ibid., p. 196.

[11] Ibid., p. 197.

[12] Ibid., p. 204.

[13] Ibid., p. 214.

[14] Ibid., p. 215.

[15] Ibid., p. 216.

[16] Ibid., p. 217.

[17] Ibid., p. 227.

[18] Ibid., p. 218.

[19] Ibid., p. 219.

[20] Ibid., pp. 229–30.

[21] Ibid., p. 229.

[22] Ibid., pp. 230, 229.

[23] Ibid., p. 229.

[24] Ibid., p. 236.

[25] Ibid., p. 237.

[26] Ibid., pp. 238, 239.

[27] Ibid., p. 239.

Pages 28–30

[1] Thomas Phillips, 'A journal of a voyage from England to Africa, and so forward to Barbadoes, in the years 1693, and 1694', in *A Collection of Voyages and Travels, some now First Printed from Original Manuscripts, others now First Published in English* (6 vols, London, 1732), VI, p. 188.

[2] R. T. W. Denning (ed.), *The Diary of William Thomas of Michaelston-super-Ely, near St Fagans, Glamorgan, 1762–1795* (Cardiff, 1995), p. 228.

[3] John Atkins, *A Voyage to Guinea, Brasil, and the West-Indies* (London, 1737), p. 61.

Pages 31–41

[1] Stephen Hughes, *Copperopolis: Landscapes of the Early Industrial Period in Swansea* (Aberystwyth, 2000), p. 45.

[2] Thomas Pennant, *The History of the Parishes of Whiteford, and Holywell* (1796), p. 203.

[3] Torsten Berg and Peter Berg (eds), *R. R. Angerstein's Illustrated Travel Diary, 1753–1755: Industry in England and Wales from a Swedish Perspective* (London, 2001), p. 324; Joan Day, *Bristol Brass: A History of the Industry* (Newton Abbot, 1973), p. 199.

[4] Pennant, *Whiteford, and Holywell*, p. 204.

[5] J. R. Harris, *The Copper King: A Biography of Thomas Williams of Llanidan* (Liverpool, 1964), p. 161.

[6] Jenny Uglow, *The Lunar Men: The Friends who Made the Future 1730–1810* (London, 2002), p. 399.

[7] Parliamentary Archives, 10/7/788, petition dated 9 July 1788.

[8] Pennant, *Whiteford, and Holywell*, p. 206.

[9] Bryan Edwards, *The History, Civil and Commercial, of the British Colonies in the West Indies* (Dublin, 1793, 2 vols), II, pp. 220–1.

[10] Ibid., p. 229.

Pages 41–5

[1] B. W. Higman, 'The sugar revolution', *Economic History Review*, 53, 2 (2000), 213.

[2] *American Husbandry; Containing an Account of the Soil, Climate, Production and Agriculture, of the British Colonies in North-America and the West-Indies* (1775), pp. 393–4.

[3] College of William and Mary, Earl Gregg Swem Library, Jerdone Family papers, MsV. 10, store daybook 1752–9.

Pages 46–54

[1] *Maryland Gazette*, 26 November 1767.

[2] Colonial Williamsburg Foundation, John D. Rockefeller, Jr Library, MS 1929.6.2, Francis Jerdone cargo wastebook, 1748–1749, entries for 24 April and 29 May 1749.

[3] T. C. Mendenhall, *The Shrewsbury Drapers and the Welsh Wool Trade in the Sixteenth and Seventeenth Centuries* (Oxford, 1953) and C. A. J. Skeel, 'The Welsh woollen industry in the sixteenth and seventeenth centuries', *Archaeologia Cambriensis*, 7th series 2 (1922), 220–58.

[4] TNA, T70/130, Committee of Goods minutes, 1703–1720.

[5] Robin Law (ed.), *The English in West Africa, 1681–1683. The Local Correspondence of the Royal African Company of England 1681–1699. Part 1* (Oxford, 1997), p. 18.

[6] Robin Law (ed.), *The English in West Africa 1681–1683. The Local Correspondence of the Royal African Company of England 1681–1699. Part 3* (Oxford, 2006), p. 3. Caboceer, the term used to denote the officials of local African states, was a corruption of *cabéceira*, the Portuguese word for head.

[7] Law, *The English in West Africa ... Part 3*, p. 260.

[8] Law, *The English in West Africa ... Part 1*, p. 237. Captain Thomas Phillips noticed the same practice at Whydah a decade later: 'they unravel most of the sayes and perpetuanoes we sell them' (Thomas Phillips, 'A journal of a voyage from England to Africa, and so forward to Barbadoes, in the years 1693, and 1694', in *A Collection of Voyages and Travels, some now First Printed from Original Manuscripts, others now First Published in English* (6 vols, London, 1732), VI), p. 220.

[9] K. G. Davies, *The Royal African Company* (London, 1957), p. 352.

[10] TNA, T70/22, 'A Scheme of Goods supposed Necessary for Stock to be on ye Gold Coast to purchase Slaves & Gold . . . 26th August 1705'.

[11] Hilary McD. Beckles, 'The "Hub of Empire": the Caribbean and Britain in the seventeenth century', in Nicholas Canny (ed.), *The Oxford History of the British Empire. Volume 1: The Origins of Empire* (Oxford, 1998), p. 224; J. R. Ward, 'The British West Indies in the age of abolition, 1748–1815', in P. J. Marshall (ed.), *The Oxford History of the British Empire. Volume 2: The Eighteenth Century* (Oxford, 1998), p. 433.

[12] Figures adapted from Ira Berlin, *Many Thousands Gone: The First Two Centuries of Slavery in North America* (Cambridge, MA, 1998), pp. 369–70. Slaves in the Mississippi valley and west Florida, areas that were subsequently absorbed into the United States but which never formed part of British North America, are excluded from the count.

[13] 'A Georgia planter buys negro clothes in London', in Ulrich B. Phillips (ed.), *Plantation and Frontier Documents: 1649–1863* (Cleveland, OH, 1909, 2 vols), I, p. 294. A similar allowance is stipulated in *American Husbandry; Containing an Account of the Soil, Climate, Production and Agriculture, of the British Colonies in North America and the West-Indies* (1775), p. 407.

[14] Lorena S. Walsh, 'Slave life, slave society, and tobacco production in the Tidewater Chesapeake, 1620–1820', in Ira Berlin and Philip D. Morgan (eds), *Cultivation and Culture: Labor and the Shaping of Slave Life in the Americas* (Charlottesville, VA, 1993), pp. 176–7.

[15] A letter of May 1732 quoted in Keith Mason, 'The world an absentee planter and his slaves made: Sir William Stapleton and his Nevis sugar estate, 1722–1740', *Bulletin of the John Rylands University Library*, 75, 1 (1993), 125–6.

[16] Thomas Pennant, *A Tour in Wales. MDCCLXX* (London, 2 vols, 1778–83), II, p. 351.

[17] 'Some notes on Green Spring. Formerly the home of Sir William Berkeley, Ludwells and Lees', *Virginia Magazine of History and Biography*, 37, 4 (October 1929), 289–300.

[18] South Caroliniana Library, University of South Carolina, Ball family papers, box 1, folder 7, Elias Ball to Elias Ball junior, 21 April 1786.

[19] Walter B. Edgar (ed.), *The Letterbook of Robert Pringle. Volume 1: April 2, 1737 – September 25, 1742* (Columbia, SC, 1972), p. xvii.

[20] *South-Carolina and American General Gazette*, 7–11 December 1770, quoted in Linda Baumgarten, *What Clothes Reveal: The Language of Clothing in Colonial and Federal America* (Williamsburg, VA, 2002), p. 136.

[21] Ibid., p. 139.

[22] Melvin Humphreys, *The Crisis of Community: Montgomeryshire, 1680–1815* (Cardiff, 1996), p. 7.

[23] George C. Rogers and David R. Chesnutt (eds), *The Papers of Henry Laurens. Volume 9: April 19, 1773 – Dec. 12, 1774* (Columbia, SC, 1981), pp. 330, 352–3.

[24] Virginia Historical Society, Mss1 C9698a, John Custis to Micajah Perry, ?1735.

[25] College of William and Mary, Earl Gregg Swem Library, Mss 39.1 J47, William Johnston to Neill Buchanan, 16 [month unclear] 1738.

[26] M. J. Jones, 'Merioneth woollen industry from 1750 to 1820', *Transactions of the Honourable Society of Cymmrodorion*, 1940 (for 1939), 193.

[27] Rhode Island Historical Society, Peace Dale Manufacturing Company Records, Mss 483 sg 36, box 1, folder 3., I. P. Hazard to D. W. Urquhart & Co, 6 June 1826. My thanks to Dr Seth Rockman of Brown University for this reference and advice on US textile manufacturers.

[28] South Caroliniana Library, University of South Carolina, Isaac Peace Hazard Papers, folder 1-legal, William Ravenel to Isaac Peace Hazard, 30 January 1832. Thanks once more to Seth Rockman.

Pages 55–7
[1] L. B. Namier, 'Anthony Bacon, M.P., an eighteenth-century merchant', in W. E. Minchinton (ed.), *Industrial South Wales 1750–1914: Essays in Welsh Economic History* (London, 1969), pp. 99–100.

Pages 58–71
[1] Charles Royster, *The Fabulous History of the Dismal Swamp Company* (New York, 2000), p. 178.

[2] L. B. Namier, 'Anthony Bacon, MP: an eighteenth-century merchant', *Journal of Economic and Business History*, 2 (1929), 80.

[3] The words of Edmund Burke, Rockingham's chief ideologist, quoted in Martyn J. Powell, 'Clerke, Sir Philip Jennings-, baronet (1722–1788)', *Oxford Dictionary of National Biography*, online edn, Oxford University Press, May 2008 (*http://www.oxforddnb.com/view/article/93442*, accessed 10 November 2008).

[4] Gloucestershire Record Office, D1086/F120, William Lewis to John Blagden Hale, 7 February 1790.

[5] M. W. Flinn (ed.), *Svedenstierna's Tour in Great Britain 1802–03: The Travel Diary of an Industrial Spy* (Newton Abbot, 1973), p. 55.

[6] Data taken from T. G. Burnard, '"Prodigious riches": the wealth of Jamaica before the American Revolution', *Economic History Review*, 54, 3 (2001), 520.

[7] Data taken from Richard S. Dunn, '"Dreadful Idlers in the Cane Fields": the slave labor pattern on a Jamaican sugar estate, 1762–1831', *Journal of Interdisciplinary History*, 17, 4 (1987), 795–822.

[8] Jean Lindsay, 'The Pennants and Jamaica 1665–1808. Part II: the economic and social development of the Pennant estates in Jamaica', *Transactions of the Caernarfonshire Historical Society*, 44 (1983), 80.

[9] Trevor Burnard, *Mastery, Tyranny, and Desire: Thomas Thistlewood and his Slaves in the Anglo-Jamaican World* (Chapel Hill, NC, 2004), p. 261.

[10] Ibid., p. 261.

[11] *Gentleman's Magazine*, XXXVI (1765), 135–6.

[12] South Caroliniana Library, University of South Carolina, Ball family papers, box 1, folder 17, Elias Ball III to Elias Ball IV, 19 January 1793.

Pages 71–2

[1] Jean Lindsay, *A History of the North Wales Slate Industry* (Newton Abbot, 1974), pp. 48, 50.

[2] University of Wales Bangor, Archives Department, Penrhyn Castle papers, 1252 and 1253, Richard Pennant to Alexander Falconer, 26 November and 10 December 1782.

[3] NLW, Tredegar Park Muniments, 64/34.

Pages 73–92

[1] George Lloyd Johnson, junior, *The Frontier in the Colonial South: South Carolina Backcountry, 1736–1800* (Westport, CT, 1997), p. 21.

[2] Thomas Bacon, *Two Sermons, Preached to a Congregation of Black Slaves, at the Parish Church of S.P. in the Province of Maryland* (London, 1749), p. 23.

[3] Ibid., p. 33.

[4] Ibid., p. v.

[5] Adam Smith, *An Inquiry into the Nature and Causes of the Wealth of Nations* (1776), ed. R. H. Campbell and A. S. Skinner (Oxford, 1976), pp. 387–8.

[6] Ibid., p. 99.

[7] Ibid., p. 388.

[8] Ibid., p. 389.

[9] Christopher Leslie Brown, *Moral Capital: Foundations of British Abolitionism* (Chapel Hill, NC, 2006), p. 219.

[10] Ibid., p. 214.

[11] Simon Schama, *Rough Crossings: Britain, the Slaves and the American Revolution* (London, 2005), p. 96.

[12] Ibid., p. 176.

[13] Adam Hochschild, *Bury the Chains: The British Struggle to Abolish Slavery* (London, 2006), p. 144.

[14] E. Wyn James, 'Welsh ballads and American slavery', *The Welsh Journal of Religious History*, 2 (2007), 62.

[15] James, 'Welsh ballads', 63.

[16] Gilbert Francklyn, *Observations, Occasioned by the Attempts Made in England to Effect the Abolition of the Slave Trade* (1789), p. 7.

[17] Gwynne E. Owen, 'Welsh anti-slavery sentiments, 1795–1865: a survey of public opinion' (unpublished MA dissertation, University of Wales, 1964), 163.

[18] College of William and Mary, Earl Gregg Swem Library, Jerdone Family papers (Mss 39.1 J47), box 2, folder 5, George Weare Braikenridge to Francis Jerdone, 13 August 1792.

[19] John T. Griffiths, *Rev. Morgan John Rhys: The Welsh Baptist Hero of Civil and Religious Liberty of the Eighteenth Century* (Carmarthen, 1910), p. 85.

[20] NLW, Tredegar Park Muniments, 64/346.

[21] Gilbert Francklyn, *An Answer to the Rev. Mr. Clarkson's Essay on the Slavery and Commerce of the Human Species* (1789), p. 89.

[22] Francklyn, *Observations*, p. 11.

[23] University College Bangor Archives, Stapleton-Cotton Manuscripts 18, Walter Nisbet to Catherine Stapleton, 23 May 1788.

[24] Roger Anstey, *The Atlantic Slave Trade and British Abolition 1760–1810* (London, 1975), p. 311.

[25] NLW, Slebech 11555, Hibbert Fuhr & Hibbert to Nathaniel Phillips, 1 July 1788.

[26] College of William and Mary, Earl Gregg Swem Library, Jerdone Family papers (Mss 39.1 J47), box 2, folder 5, George Weare Braikenridge to Francis Jerdone, 13 August 1792.

[27] Griffiths, *Morgan John Rhys*, p. 134.

[28] Ibid., p. 99.

[29] G. A. Williams, *The Search for Beulah Land: The Welsh and the Atlantic Revolution* (London, 1980), p. 82. The Book of Joshua (7: 1–26) tells how Achan looted treasure from the 'accursed' city of Jericho and so turned God against the Israelites. He and his family were stoned to death for their sin.

Pages 92–4

[1] James Epstein, 'Politics of colonial sensation: the trial of Thomas Picton and the cause of Louisa Calderon', *American Historical Review*, 112, 3 (2007), 726–7.

Pages 95–109

[1] Robert Havard, 'Picton, Sir Thomas (1758–1815)', *Oxford Dictionary of National Biography* (Oxford, 2004) (*http://www.oxforddnb.com/view/article/22219*, accessed 17 June 2009).

[2] Gelien Matthews, 'Trinidad: a model colony for British slave trade abolition', in Stephen Farrell, Melanie Unwin and James Walvin (eds), *The British Slave Trade: Abolition, Parliament and People* (Edinburgh, 2007), p. 92.

[3] James Epstein, 'The radical underworld goes colonial: P. F. McCallum's *Travels in Trinidad*', in Michael T. David and Paul Pickering (eds), *Unrespectable Radicals? Popular Politics in the Age of Reform* (Aldershot, 2008), p. 149.

[4] James Stephen, *The Crisis of the Sugar Colonies; or, An Enquiry into the Objects and Probable Effects of the French Expedition to the West Indies* (London, 1802), p. 139.

[5] Ibid., pp. 79, 80.

[6] Ibid., pp. 150–1.

[7] Ibid., pp. 161, 157.

[8] Ibid., pp. 178, 179.

[9] Ibid., p. 187.

[10] Pierre F. M'Callum, *Travels in Trinidad during the Months of February, March, and April, 1803* (Liverpool, 1805), p. 145.

[11] James Epstein, 'Politics of colonial sensation: the trial of Thomas Picton and the cause of Louisa Calderon', *American Historical Review*, 112, 3 (2007), 721.

[12] Ibid., 725.

[13] Stephen, *Crisis of the Sugar Colonies*, p. 165.

[14] Roger Anstey, *The Atlantic Slave Trade and British Abolition 1760–1810* (London, 1975), pp. 351, 352.

[15] Robin Blackburn, *The Overthrow of Colonial Slavery 1776–1848* (London, 1988), p. 310.

[16] Ibid., p. 313.

[17] Robert Harvard, *Wellington's Welsh General: A Life of Sir Thomas Picton* (London, 1996), p. 91.

Pages 109–12

[1] Gwynne E. Owen, 'Welsh anti-slavery sentiments, 1795–1865: a survey of public opinion' (unpublished MA dissertation, University of Wales, 1964), 38, 40.
[2] *Cambrian*, 11 November 1837, p. 2, col. 6.
[3] House of Commons Parliamentary Papers 1837–38 (215) vol. 48, pp. 20, 22.

Pages 113–29

[1] Peter Kolchin, *American Slavery 1619–1877* (London, 1993), p. 96.
[2] James McPherson, *Battle Cry of Freedom: The Civil War Era* (Oxford, 1988), p. 104.
[3] David R. Murray, *Odious Commerce: Britain, Spain and the Abolition of the Cuban Slave Trade* (Cambridge, 1980), pp. 18, 111.
[4] TNA, FO 453/1, consular report on the commerce of Santiago de Cuba, 3 March 1833.
[5] TNA, FO 453/1, John Hardy junior to W.S. McLeay, 23 February 1833.
[6] Ibid.
[7] David Turnbull, *Travels in the West. Cuba; With Notices of Porto Rico, and the Slave Trade* (London, 1840), p. 10.
[8] Ibid., p. 9.
[9] TNA, BT 31/1310/3371, registration documents of 11 December 1866 reciting an earlier indenture of 13 July 1835.
[10] Robin Blackburn, *The Overthrow of Colonial Slavery, 1776–1848* (London, 1988), p. 387.
[11] Turnbull, *Travels in the West*, pp. 8–9.
[12] Vicente Gonzalez Loscertales and Inés Roldán de Montaud, 'La mineria del Cobre en Cuba. Su organizacion, problemas administrativos y repercusiones socials (1828–1849)', *Revista de Indias* (1980), 275.
[13] Cornwall Record Office, AD 1341, diary of James Whitburn, 16 December 1836.
[14] Royal Institution of Cornwall, HJ1/17, Arthur Jenkins to James Poingdestre, 9 August 1837.
[15] Keith Strange, *Merthyr Tydfil, Iron Metropolis: Life in a Welsh Industrial Town* (2005), p. 170.
[16] Royal Institution of Cornwall, HJ1/16, Arthur Jenkins to William Leckie, 12 December 1835.
[17] TNA, FO 72/634, Charles Clarke to Joseph Crawford, 27 April 1843.
[18] NLW, LL/1844/181, letters of administration granted 17 June 1844.
[19] *Cambrian*, 9 February 1849.
[20] *Cambrian*, 24 October 1862.
[21] Inés Roldán de Montaud, 'Organización municipal y conflicto en la villa de El Cobre (1827–1845)', *Santiago*, 60 (1985), 124, 129.
[22] Gonzalez Loscertales and Roldán de Montaud, 'La mineria del Cobre en Cuba', 277.
[23] Turnbull, *Travels in the West*, p. 14.
[24] Samuel Hazard, *Cuba with Pen and Pencil* (1870), pp. 374–5.
[25] *Cambrian*, 20 August 1869.
[26] Bodleian Library of Commonwealth and African Studies at Rhodes House, Mss Brit. Emp. s. 22 G77, unidentified correspondent to J.H. Tredgold, 28 June 1841.
[27] *The British and Foreign Anti-Slavery Reporter*, 22 September 1841, p. 1, col. 3.

Chronology

This timeline provides some key dates in the history of Atlantic slavery. Those that feature prominently in this book are highlighted in bold.

1440   The Portuguese become the first Europeans to engage in a slave trade in sub-Saharan Africa.

c.1500 First enslaved Africans arrive in the New World.

1607   The colony of Virginia is established.

1619   Slaves are disembarked in Virginia, the first to be landed in English America.

1621   Foundation of the *Westindische Compagnie* in Amsterdam. The Dutch challenge Portugal's dominance of transatlantic slaving.

1627   The English begin the settlement of Barbados. Sugar cultivation begins in the 1640s, leading to the mass importation of Africans.

1655   The English invade Jamaica. Initially used as privateering base, the island switches to slave-based plantation agriculture in the 1670s and 1680s.

1663   Foundation of the Royal African Company.

1668   **Henry Morgan captures Portobello. The destruction of Panama follows in 1671.**

1670   The colony of South Carolina is founded.

1688   **Death of Henry Morgan. The ex-privateer is owner of Llanrumney plantation on Jamaica's north coast.**

1680s Heavy importation of Africans into Virginia gets underway.

1690s **Coal-fired copper smelting begins in the Neath district.**

1693   **The *Hannibal* sails from London under the command of Captain Thomas Phillips. She loads with slaves for the Royal African Company.**

1697   Treaty of Ryswick ends the Nine Years War. France is granted the western half of the island of Hispaniola. The new colony is named Saint-Domingue.

1698   The Royal African Company's monopoly of trade with Guinea is withdrawn. Private traders from London and Bristol sweep into the slaving business and the British become the foremost slavers in the Atlantic world.

1700s   Enslaved Africans begin to flood into South Carolina.

1713   The Treaty of Utrecht ends the War of Spanish Succession. The Royal African Company is awarded the exclusive contract to supply slaves to the Spanish empire.

1717   **First copper smelter in the Swansea valley built at Llangyfelach.**

1730s   **The Coster family establishes the White Rock copper works near Swansea. They invest simultaneously in slaving expeditions from Bristol.**

1758   The British capture France's Senegalese forts in the early stages of the Seven Years War.

1760s   **Copper ore is discovered at Parys Mountain on Anglesey.**

1762   **William Williams Pantycelyn begins publication of *Pantheologia*. Williams subsequently publishes a Welsh translation of *A narrative of the most remarkable particulars in the life of James Albert Ukawsaw Gronniosaw, an African prince*, one of the first written accounts of the Middle Passage by a survivor.**

1763   Treaty of Paris concludes the Seven Years War. France cedes several of her Caribbean possessions to Britain.

1766   **Anthony Bacon begins the construction of the Cyfarthfa ironworks.**

1772   **Maurice Morgann publishes *Plan for the abolition of slavery in the West Indies*, the first concrete proposal for slave emancipation in the British empire.**

1775   Outbreak of the American Revolution. Lord Dunmore, royal governor of Virginia, promises freedom to the slaves of rebel masters who will enlist with the British.

1780s   **Thomas Williams of Llanidan monopolises copper ore extraction in Britain.**
Measures to bring about the gradual emancipation of slaves are introduced in most of the northern states of the new American Republic.

1782 **Richard Pennant inherits his family's Jamaican plan-tations. He begins the development of the Penrhyn slate quarry.**

1783 Black British army veterans are evacuated from the new United States and resettled in Nova Scotia.

1787 Foundation of the Committee for Effecting an Abolition of the Slave Trade.
The first fleet carrying ex-slave soldiers sets out for the free labour colony in Sierra Leone.

1788 First mass petitioning movement in Britain against the slave trade. Formation of the *Société des Amis des Noirs* in France.

1789 The outbreak of the French Revolution begins the unrav-elling of the social and racial order in France's sugar colonies. **Baptist minister Morgan John Rhys begins to polemicise against slavery.**

1791 Slave insurrection in Saint-Domingue.

1792 Overthrow of the French monarchy.

1793 The new French Republic declares war on Britain. The abolitionist cause suffers as the Republic adopts a policy of revolutionary emancipation for colonial slaves.

1794 Suppression of domestic radicalism in Britain. **Morgan John Rhys emigrates to the United States.**

1797 **The British capture the Spanish island of Trinidad. Thomas Picton is appointed military governor.**

1800s Cuban sugar production begins its dramatic early nine-teenth-century expansion.

1800 **Wales produces 41 per cent of the global output of smelted copper.**

1802 James Stephen publishes *The Crisis of the Sugar Colonies* (1802).
Napoleon restores French colonial slavery.

1804 Foundation of the Republic of Haiti.

1806 **Trial of Thomas Picton for his actions as governor of Trinidad.**
Foreign Slave Trade Act prevents British shippers sup-plying slaves to non-British territories.

1807 Abolition of the British slave trade.

146

1808   Prohibition of slave imports into the United States.

1815   **Sir Thomas Picton dies at the battle of Waterloo.**

1820s Slave-based cotton growing extends rapidly across the American south-west.
Slave importation into Brazil reaches its zenith.

1823   Foundation of the Society for the Mitigation and Gradual Abolition of Slavery.
Slave rebellion in Demerara.

1830s **British mining companies revive copper ore extraction at El Cobre in Cuba using slave labour.**

1831   Slave rebellion in Jamaica: the 'Baptist War'.

1832   Great Reform Act permanently alters the parliamentary arithmetic in Britain and opens the way for slave emancipation.

1834   Slavery abolished in the British West Indies.

1838   The ending of 'apprenticeship' in the British sugar colonies brings about final emancipation for ex-slaves.

1843   **Act for the more effectual Suppression of the Slave Trade is passed. Slave-holding by British mining companies is outlawed but the law is easily evaded.**

1848   Abolition of slavery in the colonies of France.

1850   British diplomacy and naval aggression ends the importation of slaves to Brazil.

1861   Outbreak of the American Civil War.

1865   After the defeat of the Confederacy the Thirteenth Amendment to the US Constitution abolishes slavery.

1866   Last known landing of African slaves in the Americas takes place in Cuba.

1868   Ten Years War in Cuba paves the way for emancipation in the Spanish colonial world.

1888   The emancipation of all slaves in Brazil is decreed.

Guide to Further Reading

General works on the slave trade and Atlantic slavery

Ira Berlin, *Many Thousands Gone: The First Two Centuries of Slavery in North America* (Cambridge, MA, 1998)

Robin Blackburn, *The Making of New World Slavery: From the Baroque to the Modern 1492–1800* (London, 1997)

Stanley Engermann, Seymour Drescher and Robert Paquette (eds), *Slavery* (Oxford, 2001)

Herbert S. Klein, *The Atlantic Slave Trade* (Cambridge, 1999)

Peter Kolchin, *American Slavery 1619–1877* (London, 1993)

Hugh Thomas, *The Slave Trade: The History of the Atlantic Slave Trade 1440–1870* (London, 1997)

John Thornton, *Africa and Africans in the Making of the Atlantic World, 1400–1800* (Cambridge, 1998)

The Royal African Company

K. G. Davies, *The Royal African Company* (London, 1957)

Robin Law (ed.), *The English in West Africa: The Local Correspondence of the Royal African Company of England 1681–1699.* (Oxford, 1997–2006)

William St Clair, *The Grand Slave Emporium: Cape Coast Castle and the British Slave Trade* (London, 2006)

The Middle Passage

Marcus Rediker, *The Slave Ship: A Human History* (London, 2007)

Stephanie E. Smallwood, *Saltwater Slavery: A Middle Passage from Africa to American Diaspora* (Cambridge, MA, 2007)

The plantation

Trevor Burnard, *Mastery, Tyranny, and Desire: Thomas Thistlewood and his Slaves in the Anglo-Jamaican World* (Chapel Hill, NC, 2004)

S. Max Edelson, *Plantation Enterprise in Colonial South Carolina* (Cambridge, MA, 2006)

Philip D. Morgan, *Slave Counterpoint: Black Culture in the Eighteenth-Century Chesapeake and Lowcountry* (Chapel Hill, NC, 1998)

Lorena S. Walsh, *From Calabar to Carter's Grove: The History of a Virginia Slave Community* (Charlottesville, VA, 1997)

Anthony Bacon

Chris Evans, *The Labyrinth of Flames: Work and Social Conflict in Early Industrial Merthyr Tydfil* (Cardiff, 1993)

L. B. Namier, 'Anthony Bacon, MP: an eighteenth-century merchant', *Journal of Economic and Business History*, 2 (1929), 20–70

David Richardson and M. M. Schofield, 'Whitehaven and the eighteenth-century British slave trade', *Transactions of the Cumberland and Westmoreland Antiquarian and Archaeological Society*, 92 (1992), 183–204

Charles Royster, *The Fabulous History of the Dismal Swamp Company* (New York, 2000)

The Pennants and the North Wales slate industry

Jean Lindsay, 'The Pennants and Jamaica 1665–1808. Part I: The growth and organisation of the Pennant estates', *Transactions of the Caernarfonshire Historical Society*, 43 (1982), 37–82

Jean Lindsay, 'The Pennants and Jamaica 1665–1808. Part II: The economic and social development of the Pennant estates in Jamaica', *Transactions of the Caernarfonshire Historical Society*, 44 (1983), 59–96

Copper as a trade good

Joan Day, *Bristol Brass: A History of the Industry* (Newton Abbot, 1973)

J. R. Harris, *The Copper King: A Biography of Thomas Williams of Llanidan* (Liverpool, 1964)

Eugenia W. Herbert, *Red Gold of Africa: Copper in Pre-colonial History and Culture* (Madison, WI, 2003)

Stephen Hughes, *Copperopolis: Landscapes of the Early Industrial Period in Swansea* (Aberystwyth, 2000)

David Richardson, 'West African consumption patterns and their influence on the eighteenth-century English slave trade', in Henry A. Gemery and Jan S. Henderson (eds), *The Uncommon Market: Essays in the Economic History of the Atlantic Slave Trade* (New York, 1979), pp. 303–30

Abolition

Roger Anstey, *The Atlantic Slave Trade and British Abolition 1760–1810* (London, 1975)

Robin Blackburn, *The Overthrow of Colonial Slavery 1776–1848* (London, 1988)

Christopher Leslie Brown, *Moral Capital: Foundations of British Abolitionism* (Chapel Hill, NC, 2006)

David Brion Davies, *The Problem of Slavery in the Age of Revolution 1770–1823* (Oxford, 1999)

Seymour Drescher, *From Slavery to Freedom: Comparative Studies in the Rise and Fall of Atlantic Slavery* (Basingstoke, 1999)

Adam Hochschild, *Bury the Chains: The British Struggle to Abolish Slavery* (London, 2006)

John R. Oldfield, *Popular Politics and British Anti-Slavery: The Mobilisation of Public Opinion against the Slave Trade, 1787–1807* (London, 1998)

Simon Schama, *Rough Crossings: Britain, the Slaves and the American Revolution* (London, 2005)

Saint-Domingue – Haiti

Lauren Dubois, *Avengers of the New World: The Story of the Haitian Revolution* (Cambridge, MA, 2004)

David P. Geggus, *The Impact of the Haitian Revolution in the Atlantic World* (Columbia, SC, 2001)

C. L. R. James, *The Black Jacobins: Toussaint L'Ouverture and the San Domingo Revolution* (London, 2001)

Franklin Knight, 'The Haitian Revolution', *American Historical Review*, 105, 1 (2000), 103–15

Trinidad

James Epstein, 'Politics of colonial sensation: the trial of Thomas Picton and the cause of Louisa Calderon', *American Historical Review*, 112, 3 (2007), 712–41

Robert Harvard, *Wellington's Welsh General: A Life of Sir Thomas Picton* (London, 1996)

Gelien Matthews, 'Trinidad: a model colony for British slave trade abolition', in Stephen Farrell, Melanie Unwin and James Walvin (eds), *The British Slave Trade: Abolition, Parliament and People* (Edinburgh, 2007), pp. 84–96

Cuban slavery and Swansea copper

David R. Murray, *Odious Commerce: Britain, Spain and the Abolition of the Cuban Slave Trade* (Cambridge, 1980)

Edmund Newell, '"Copperopolis": the rise and fall of the copper industry in the Swansea district, 1826–1921', *Business History*, 32, 3 (1990), 75–97

Dale Tomich, 'World Slavery and Caribbean Capitalism: The Cuban Sugar Industry, 1760–1868', *Theory and Society*, 20, 3 (1991), 297–319

Local studies

Madge Dresser, *Slavery Obscured: The Social History of the Slave Trade in an English Provincial Port* (London, 2001), which deals with Bristol.

David Richardson, 'Slavery and Bristol's "Golden Age"', *Slavery and Abolition*, 26 (2005), 35–45

David Richardson, Anthony Tibbles and Suzanne Schwarz (eds), *Liverpool and Transatlantic Slavery* (Liverpool, 2007)

Nini Rodgers, *Ireland, Slavery and Anti-Slavery: 1612–1865* (Basingstoke, 2007)

Iain Whyte, *Scotland and the Abolition of Black Slavery, 1756–1838* (Edinburgh, 2006)

The legacy of Atlantic slavery

Joseph E. Inikori, *Africans and the Industrial Revolution in England: A Study in International Trade and Economic Development* (Cambridge, 2002)

Kenneth Morgan, *Slavery, Atlantic Trade and the British Economy, 1660–1800* (Cambridge, 2000)

Barbara L. Solow and Stanley L. Engerman (eds), *British Capitalism and Caribbean Slavery: The Legacy of Eric Williams* (Cambridge, 1987)

Eric Williams, *Capitalism and Slavery* (Chapel Hill, NC, 1944)

Index